Louise Bogan

Twayne's United States Authors Series

Warren French, Editor
Indiana University, Indianapolis

TUSAS 461

LOUISE BOGAN
(1897–1970)
Photograph courtesy of
Alfred A. Knopf, Inc.

Louise Bogan

By Jaqueline Ridgeway

Marquette University

Twayne Publishers • Boston

Louise Bogan

Jaqueline Ridgeway

Copyright © 1984 by G. K. Hall & Company
All Rights Reserved
Published by Twayne Publishers
A Division of G. K. Hall & Company
70 Lincoln Street
Boston, Massachusetts 02111

Book Production by Elizabeth Todesco

Book Design by Barbara Anderson

Printed on permanent/durable acid-free
paper and bound in the United States of
America.

**Library of Congress Cataloging in
Publication Data.**

Ridgeway, Jaqueline.
    Louise Bogan.

    (Twayne's United States authors series; TUSAS 461)
    Bibliography: p. 139
    Includes index.
    1. Bogan, Louise, 1897–1970—
Criticism and interpretation.
I. Title.   II. Series.
PS3503.O195Z84   1984   811'.52   84-10931
ISBN 0-8057-7401-7

Contents

About the Author

Jaqueline Ridgeway received her Ph.D. in English at the University of California, Riverside, in 1977 with a major in twentieth-century American and British literature. Since then she has taught English, both composition and literature, as a lecturer at the University of California, Riverside, and at the University of Nevada, Reno. She is now teaching classes at several colleges in Wisconsin.

Preface

Louise Bogan, who lived from 1897 to 1970, made a distinguished contribution to American poetry both in her poems themselves and in her influence on other poets which, though honored, has not been adequately recognized. The literary circumstances that contributed to this lack of recognition are the very ones that make it important to investigate the nature of her work. For in a period when many of her contemporaries were questioning and often abandoning formal poetic traditions, she kept to a centuries-old mainstream of values in seeing poetry as fulfilling a psychological need to express the inexpressible through the formal components of meter and stanza, because poetic form, like music, has a physiological basis. At the same time, recognizing that language and ways of thinking and feeling change, she used meter and stanza in direct expression of these changes. Form was poetic necessity to Bogan, not convention, and she felt no need to rebel against it.

In a body of poetry that is small but vital, she achieved a concentration of meaning in a lyrical mode that helped to validate the surviving authenticity of lyric poetry. Inspired by her poetry, younger poets, especially Theodore Roethke, were encouraged to find their own voices in the lyric mode.

Although esteemed by fellow poets, Bogan has not had a wide audience, principally because her poetry is not always easy to understand. Her work often is an expression of the subconscious, manifested in symbols not immediately available to a simple interpretation. I hope, in this investigation of the poetry, to illuminate to some extent the meanings of these symbols and the overall nature of her poetic statement. Her poetry, in its complexity, will continue, as Roethke once said, to yield new meanings, but I have attempted to indicate the significance of early childhood events upon her life view as well as the sophistication of her sense of universal pattern.

I have not attempted to include discussion of Bogan's translations of poetry from foreign languages. I have included a chapter on her short stories only to analyze themes that bear upon her poetry. After the first two chapters, which concern the overall form and genre of the poetry, I have organized the chapters in the chronological order of her poetry, beginning with very early poems and continuing with her published books of poetry. I have done this because each book represents a culmination of life experience reflected in its poems. For the same reason, rather than to concentrate upon the major poems, I have chosen to deal with her poetry as a whole in order to show the interrelationships that contribute to the major themes.

The reactions of critics and others to Bogan's poetry, from the time of publication to the present, is touched upon in the conclusion in the process of placing her poetic accomplishment in continuing perspective.

Jaqueline Ridgeway

Marquette University

Acknowledgments

Grateful acknowledgment is made to Farrar, Straus and Giroux, Inc., for permission to reprint from *The Blue Estuaries* by Louise Bogan. Copyright 1923, 1929, 1930, 1931, 1933, 1934, 1935, 1937, 1938, 1941, 1949, 1951, 1952, 1954, 1957, © 1958, 1962, 1963, 1964, 1965, 1966, 1967, 1968 by Louise Bogan. All rights reserved.

Excerpts from *What the Woman Lived: Selected Letters of Louise Bogan 1920–1970,* edited by Ruth Limmer, are reprinted by permission of Harcourt Brace Jovanovich, Inc., © 1973 by Ruth Limmer, Trustee, Estate of Louise Bogan.

Excerpts from *A Poet's Alphabet: Reflections on the Literary Art and Vocation* by Louise Bogan, edited by Robert Phelps and Ruth Limmer, are reprinted by permission of Ruth Limmer, Trustee, Estate of Louise Bogan.

Excerpts from *Journey Around My Room: The Autobiography of Louise Bogan,* A Mosaic by Ruth Limmer, © 1980 by Ruth Limmer, are reprinted by permission of Viking Penguin, Inc. Portions of this work were originally published in the *New Yorker.*

Excerpts from "The Situation in American Writing: Seven Questions (Part Two)," *Partisan Review,* are reprinted by permission of Ruth Limmer, Trustee, Estate of Louise Bogan. The lines from "Untitled" by Louise Bogan, first published in *Poetry,* copyright October 1937 by The Modern Poetry Association, are reprinted by permission of the editor of *Poetry* and of Ruth Limmer, Trustee, Estate of Louise Bogan.

Excerpts from the short stories, "Hydrotherapy," "Sunday at Five," "The Last Tear," "The Short Life of Emily," and "Zest," and from the poems, "Old Divinity," "Hidden," and "For an Old Dance," are from short stories and poems originally published in the *New Yorker* and reprinted by permission of Ruth Limmer, Trustee, Estate of Louise Bogan.

Grateful acknowledgment is made to Boston University Libraries, Special Collections, for permission to reprint "The Betrothal of King Cophetua" by Louise Bogan from the *Anthology of Boston University Poetry.*

Reprinted with permission of Macmillan Publishing Co., Inc., from the *Collected Poems* of William Butler Yeats are the lines from "Shepherd and Goatherd" and "The Wild Swans at Coole," copyright 1919 by Macmillan Publishing Co., Inc., renewed 1947 by Bertha Georgie Yeats; the words from "The Dolls" and notes to the poem, copyright 1916 by Macmillan Publishing Co., Inc., renewed 1944 by Bertha Georgie Yeats; and the lines from "The Mask," copyright 1912 by Macmillan Publishing Co., Inc., renewed 1940 by Bertha Georgie Yeats.

Excerpts from the Louise Bogan Papers in the Amherst College Library are reprinted by permission of the Trustees of Amherst College and of Ruth Limmer, Trustee, Estate of Louise Bogan.

Grateful acknowledgment is made to the New York Public Library, the Berg Collection, for excerpts from the Letters to May Sarton, reprinted by permission of Ruth Limmer, Trustee, Estate of Louise Bogan.

Grateful acknowledgment is made to the Joseph Regenstein Library of the University of Chicago, Special Collections, for permission to publish excerpts from the *Poetry* Magazine Papers (1912–1936) and to Ruth Limmer, Trustee, Estate of Louise Bogan.

I am grateful to the Recorded Sound Division of the Library of Congress for making available to me the tapes of Louise Bogan reading her poetry.

I am grateful to Maidie Alexander Scannell for assistance in gaining access to the Berg Collection and for a very pleasant conversation in New York City, and to Ruth Limmer for continued assistance over several years.

Chapter 1 of this book is a slightly changed and expanded version of an article I wrote, "The Necessity of Form to the Poetry of Louise Bogan," for *Women's Studies* 5, no. 2 (1977), issue edited by Gloria Bowles.

I am grateful to Professor Warren French for his support and encouragement.

Chronology

1950 *Works in the Humanities Published in Great Britain, 1939–1946.*

1951 *Achievement in American Poetry, 1900–1950.*

1952 Becomes a member of the National Institute of Arts and Letters. Spring, visiting professor at the University of Arkansas.

1954 *Collected Poems 1923–1953.*

1955 *Selected Criticism: Poetry and Prose.* Shares the Bollingen Prize with Léonie Adams.

1958 Lecturer at the Salzburg Seminar in American Studies, Salzburg, Austria.

1959 Award from the Academy of American Poets for her distinguished contribution to American poetry.

1960 Translation of *The Glass Bees* by Ernest Jünger (with Elizabeth Mayer). Spring, visiting professor at the University of Washington.

1963 Translation of Goethe's *Elective Affinities* (with Elizabeth Mayer).

1964 Translation of *The Journal of Jules Renard* (with Elizabeth Roget).

1964–1965 Visiting professor at Brandeis University.

1965 *The Golden Journey: Poems for Young People* (anthology with William Jay Smith).

1967 National Endowment for the Arts Award.

1968 *The Blue Estuaries: Poems 1923–1968.*

1969 Elected to the American Academy of Arts and Letters. Retires from *New Yorker.*

1970 Dies February 4. *A Poet's Alphabet: Reflections on the Literary Art and Vocation,* published posthumously.

1971 Translation of Goethe's *The Sorrows of Young Werther and Novella,* published posthumously.

Chapter One
The Necessity of Form to the Poetry of Louise Bogan

A Definition of Form

Louise Bogan wrote an article in 1953 entitled "The Pleasures of Formal Poetry" in which she defined both what she meant by formal poetry and what she thought its function and importance to be: "What is formal poetry? It is poetry written in form. And what is *form*? The elements of form, so far as poetry is concerned, arc meter and rhyme."[1] After reviewing the history of meter and rhyme and discussing their basic connection with physiological rhythms, she said that poetic patterns fell into disfavor when they no longer arose from the spoken language of the poet and the emotions prompting the writing. Change in pattern is necessary, she said, but "a failure in any discoverable beat is a failure in tension."[2]

I think a statement Bogan quotes from Gilbert Murray—"Poetry tries to convey truth concerning those subjects about which we care most and know least, or at any rate are least able to make explicit statements"—is important in understanding the function of form in Bogan's poetry.[3] The fact that for her rhythmic elements constituted form, and that they served to express the otherwise inexpressible, ties poetic form very closely to musical form. Bogan often used musical terms and metaphors in her poetry and indicated by notes on manuscripts and by comment that she thought of some of her lyrics as being accompanied by music.[4]

Susanne K. Langer, in *Feeling and Form,* describes the relationship of music to the human mind or psychology:

The tonal structures we call "music" bear a close logical similarity to the forms of human feeling—forms of growth and of attenuation, flowing and stowing, conflict and resolution, speed, arrest, terrific excitement, calm, or subtle activation and dreamy lapses—not joy and sorrow perhaps, but the poignancy of either and both—the greatness and brevity and eternal passing

I

of everything vitally felt. Such is the pattern, or logical form, of sentience; and the pattern of music is that same form worked out in pure, measured sound and silence. Music is a tonal analogue of emotive life.

Such formal analogy, or congruence of logical structures, is the prime requisite for the relation between a symbol and whatever it is to mean.[5]

She offers a definition of all art, not just music, as a basis for the content of her book: "Art is the creation of forms symbolic of human feeling" (p. 40).

It is a definition that agrees with Bogan's views of art. Bogan never used the traditional forms in a merely conventional way simply because they were traditional. She used meter and rhyme (when she used rhyme) for their original, traditional purpose of paralleling the rhythms of human feeling and always in a manner that arose from the demands of the poem.

Form in Life

Form is also an attempt to pattern, to see meaning. Human feeling is less directly behind this kind of form because it represents an ordering of feeling rather than a direct expression, a response to feeling. In dealing with feelings not directly understood, this response can be fear and the other negative emotions associated with fear. Bogan evidenced this necessity for form, too. She wrote Rolfe Humphries in 1938, "I think, in bed in the mornings, of the terrible things my insistence upon form in life has done to me and to others."[6] On the other hand, the impulse to order, to contain the chaotic was expressed in a letter written in 1966: "It *is* difficult to see the world run by anything *but* a demon (the universe, too). The only hope is: that there must be an edge (a sort of *selvage*) of good, that holds and defines."[7]

Given this need both to express and to contain the unknowable, Bogan, although writing in a period when many American poets were rejecting conventional form, wrote poetry that is formal. It had to be to express what she had to say, for her poetry deals with a struggle for meaning in a life bound by form. This is not to say that she was not an artist with a sense of self and the courage to fight for that self or that she was not the independent thinker that she was; but she had been reared in the traditional authoritarian institutions of church and family and, either as a result or in addition, had a built-in sense of order that her sense of self had to reckon with.

For her, any revolt had to be in terms of this order, as her poetry says. Societal forms like literary forms impose a meaning that must be struggled against yet used and redefined to achieve a new meaning. Bogan was largely aware of some of the aspects of this struggle—those that dealt with church, family, and class attitudes—and credited them with shaping her poetry. But there were other aspects that shaped her poetry, it seems to me, even more because she was unaware of them. However, let us consider first the former. In an interview for the *Partisan Review* in 1939, Bogan responded in part to the question "Are you conscious, in your writing, of the existence of a 'usable past'?" with the following remarks:

> Because what education I received came from New England schools, before 1916, my usable past has more of a classic basis than it would have today, even in the same background. The courses in English Literature which I encountered during my secondary education and one year of college, were not very nutritious. But my "classical" education was severe, and I read Latin prose and poetry and Xenophon and the Iliad, during my adolescence.[8]

To the question, in the same interview, "Do you find, in retrospect, that your writing reveals any allegiance to any group, class, organization, region, religion, or system of thought, or do you conceive of it as mainly the expression of yourself as an individual?" she responded by discussing "allegiances" in terms of the effects upon her writing of the circumstances of her life: the "real liturgy" of the Roman Catholic church, her Celtic heritage to which she attributed a gift for language, the unusual energy of her mother's family, and her classical education. However, she also described the traumatic effects of being considered always as an Irish Catholic in a society of Anglo-Saxon Protestants:

> It was borne in upon me, all during my adolescence, that I was a "Mick," no matter what my other faults or virtues might be. It took me a long time to take this fact easily, and to understand the situation which gave rise to the minor persecutions I endured at the hands of supposedly educated and humane people.

Coming from what she described as the white-collar class, she struggled against class prejudices that favored social respectability and status, that admired "nice people." ("These tendencies I have wrung out of my spiritual constitution with a great deal of success, I am proud to say.") She concludes her answer to the overall question by saying, "Beyond these basic influences, I think of my writing as the expression of my own development as an individual."[9]

Her letters shed further light on the influences of church and family. In a letter to Rolfe Humphries in 1938, she made a remark that suggests that the emotional nature of her response to the Catholic church had other elements than appreciation of the liturgy:

You and I are evidently working out our respective Karmas in opposite directions. I began with *The Sacred Heart Messenger* and was often told that if I went into a Protestant Church I should suffer the spiritual equivalent of having my ears drop off. You are ending under authority; and *next* time we live, maybe we can have some sense and some fun.[10]

Her feelings toward her mother were mixed, as well. She wrote Allen Tate in 1941, "I never cared for the Bogans. . . . all my talent comes from my mother's side."[11] But in a letter to Edmund Wilson in 1939, she suggested an inheritance from the other side of her family working in opposition to her mother's qualities—an unimaginative, rigidly mundane quality that Yeats attributed to the uncultured class of Irish:

I made a visit to my own ancestral home, and am beginning to understand more and more what Yeats meant by "Paudeen," and why my mother was an admirable person, even if she nearly wrecked every ordinary life within sight.—She was against the penny-pinchers and the logic-choppers; she loved beauty and threw everything away, and, what is most important, she was filled with the strongest vitality I have ever seen.—And how the "Paudeens" (from which the other side of my nature unfortunately stems!) hated and feared her![12]

In an earlier letter, one to Rolfe Humphries in 1924, she had said that her life was "blighted *very* early" by a strong, dominating mother,[13] and in a much later letter to May Sarton (April 2, 1954), she discussed her mother in terms of her poetry:

It is difficult for me to sum up briefly what I meant about my mother experience. There are certain phases of this experience which I have never told anyone, and never shall. Let me only say that it was too much, and it lasted too long—right through my life up until the age of 39. The most poignant and enduring things in the relationship are in my poetry. The rest exhausted me forever.[14]

Bogan consciously fought against the confining aspects of church and family while keeping the appreciation of form they had instilled in her: the liturgy of the Roman Catholic church and her mother's love of beauty and logic (that is, what Bogan saw as her mother's rejection of "logic-choppers"). Given this early beginning, her education in the Boston Girls' Latin School reinforced her love of form by instructing her in the classics. Even her experience as a "Mick" in Boston was an experience in form, that of social hierarchy—a form that she felt it necessary to resist, however. But though she resisted social categorizing, she felt enough of the tendency in herself to feel that she had "wrung it out."

The Dilemma of the Woman Poet

Nevertheless, her poetry and criticism reveal that there was another kind of social categorizing that she never succeeded in wringing out. And that is the categorizing of sex roles. Both as an artist and as a woman, she assimilated certain societal attitudes toward women that operated in direct conflict with her innermost desires for expression and development in art and in life.

In art, she saw women as somehow less than men, one feels. Although she defended the contribution of women poets from Sappho to the modern day, she considered the talent of women to be chiefly lyrical ("In women, more than in men, the intensity of their emotions is the key to the treasures of their spirit.")[15] She realized to some extent the hampering role that society played in the development of women artists and, as she grew older, seemed to acknowledge the increasing diversity of achievement of women poets; but as late as 1963 in a book review entitled "No Poétesses Maudites: May Swenson, Anne Sexton," she was still saying:

But beneath surface likenesses, women's poetry continues to be unlike men's, all feminist statements to the contrary notwithstanding. Women function differently, in art as in life, and it should be an enlivening rather than a dismal fact that there are some things they either cannot or are unwilling to do, and others that they do very badly.[16]

6 LOUISE BOGAN

What is relevant here, I suggest, is not that Bogan believes women poets to be essentially different from men poets (even as many questions and arguments spring to mind) but that she says so in such a negative manner, even though the things that she proceeds to say women cannot do—be rough, "totally abandoned or directly destructive," "throw reason to the winds," be a Surrealist with its harshnesses, or a poétess maudite—are not the things she admires. On the conscious level, she respects the accomplishment of women. On the unconscious level, she incorporates society's lack of expectation of their accomplishment. This basic feeling must have been a force to be reckoned with in her own view of herself as an artist, and undoubtedly contributed to the high standards and ruthless self-criticism that caused her to reprint only 105 poems in her last volume of collected poems, *The Blue Estuaries* (1968).

Her view of herself as a woman, of course, is part of this ambivalence and is shown in her poems dealing with love between men and women. Nowhere in such poems is there a woman as persona who can happily be herself in a relationship with a man. The persona's existence as an individual seems in jeopardy in love. Only by accepting loneliness can she be free. She is fiercely independent and at the same time painfully aware of the lack of communication between the sexes; but it does not seem to occur to her that this situation is other than ordained by nature—another authority.[17]

The Conflict Contained in Symbol and Form

It is this constant conflict between will and authority that shapes Bogan's poems.[18] Because she herself unconsciously represented some of the strictures her spirit rebelled against, only form and symbol can express the tight, concentrated emotions of the unconscious struggling with the conscious.[19] Although she strove always to make her poetry something beyond the narrowly personal and to cast out "small emotions with which poetry should not, and cannot deal,"[20] to be objective (a note on the worksheet indicating the poems to be published in the volume *The Sleeping Fury* says "they must be as objective as possible"),[21] it is often the personal emotion of the poet that informs the poem and gives authenticity to it. The emotion which is distanced by formal structures, sometimes distanced to the point of a "mask," a male persona, operates to illustrate the inherent conflict that the poem is really about.

For example, the first poem in all but two of her volumes of poetry (*Dark Summer* and *The Sleeping Fury* which did not repeat previous poems) is "A Tale," in which the protagonist is male and the goal becomes estranging and dangerous. That Bogan visualized the quester as male masks the feminine poet's voice as the imagery masks the precise nature of the quest. I believe that Bogan chose this poem as an introduction to her poetry because it expresses her poetic impetus, her aspiration toward significance and beauty in the face of mutability and human limitation. Its concentrated, somewhat obscure symbolism contains her personal pain and fear in a form that could signify any pain or fear and thereby hides hers. The nightmare quality of ". . . south / Of hidden deserts, torn fire glares / On beauty with a rusted mouth" is that of the irrational danger of dream with the personification of "torn fire glares." The danger is that of an elemental threat to "beauty"—to the longing for meaning, the fulfillment of life or more than life—the threat that everyday existence brings. Bogan's concerns with the sound and meaning of language and with the function of form are exemplified, as well, in this poem.

> This youth too long has heard the break
> Of waters in a land of change.
> He goes to see what suns can make
> From soil more indurate and strange.
>
> He cuts what holds his days together
> And shuts him in, as lock on lock:
> The arrowed vane announcing weather,
> The tripping racket of a clock;
>
> Seeking, I think, a light that waits
> Still as a lamp upon a shelf,—
> A land with hills like rocky gates
> Where no sea leaps upon itself.
>
> But he will find that nothing dares
> To be enduring, save where, south
> Of hidden deserts, torn fire glares
> On beauty with a rusted mouth,—
>
> Where something dreadful and another
> Look quietly upon each other.[22]

The title, "A Tale," immediately makes available a mythic hero, a
"youth," who can dare severe hardship for a tantalizing prize, but the
close correlation between verbal meaning and form produces an emotional atmosphere of yearning and fear. Within an iambic tetrameter,
abab stanza pattern, a great variation in aural line length and emphasis reflects the concentrated meaning of the words: the fast, short
lines of the first two stanzas building to the harsh "The tripping
racket of a clock" suggest a desperation, a struggle against confine-
ment, that belies strength—or at least confidence in strength. The
poem is moved beyond a "tale" to a denser symbolism. The conventional stanza form and regular rhythm and rhyme scheme create a
pattern of the inevitability of time and season that "shuts him in,"
while the impact of the words creates a strong tension against it.

I suggest that the youth as a symbol of something more than the
traditional male quest becomes apparent by the intrusion of the poet
in the third stanza with the line "Seeking, *I* think, a light that waits"
(my italic). The movement becomes slower and the tone more considered as though checking the momentum of the foregoing stanzas. The
goal is "a light that waits / Still as a lamp upon a shelf,—" beyond
the danger of time and change. The imagery of light suggests the
light of the mind, of inspiration, of knowledge or larger meaning—
a significance beyond the daily and the mutable. This stanza, in the
middle of the poem, is the only one to bring the poet to the forefront
as more than narrator and is the one in which the goal, however
symbolically, is defined not by the youth but by the poet.

It is a goal gained in safety. The actuality, however, is different;
and in the next stanza the emphasis is again on "he" but the dangers
are neither vanquished nor understood. All the ambiguities of aspiration in conjunction with the fear of the price are climaxed in the
solemn, rhymed concluding couplet: "Where something dreadful and
another / Look quietly upon each other."

A less complicated poem, a little lyric called "Song" in Bogan's
first published volume of poetry, *Body of This Death,* affords a more
obvious illustration of the use of form to carry an emotion unable to
be expressed more directly:

> Love me because I am lost;
> Love me that I am undone.
> That is brave,—no man has wished it,
> Not one.

> Be strong, to look on my heart
> As others look on my face.
> Love me,—I tell you that it is a ravaged
> Terrible place.[23]

Here, form intensifies the irony and bitterness of the words. That no man has wished to love her for herself as a complex, troubled person is too painful to say without attempting the satire of a love song. The light rhythm of the first two lines in each stanza and the repetition of "Love me" is in contrast to the interrupted, harsher rhythm of the third and fourth lines that convey the bleakest words. Only a person who feels that the world cannot regard the pain seriously makes a "song" of such a subject. Agony does not make for satire, and Bogan realized later that something was wrong with the poem (she avoided what the poem was saying, however, in deciding that it might be "mawkish") and did not reprint it.[24]

Although she chose to drop this poem, in others she treated much the same subject with increased complexity of idea and form. "Fifteenth Farewell" uses a double Italian sonnet to mirror the play of mind upon feeling. The tightly interrelated thought, rhyme, and movement of line dignify by objectification the rejection of an unsatisfactory relationship. The music of the lines reflects the underlying poignancy of the subject; but in the close correlation of consonance, assonance, and rhyme to the meaning of the words, the effect of the poem is unified to a more distanced emotion—to reflection upon the emotion. For instance, in the first three lines of the poem ("You may have all things from me, save my breath, / The slight life in my throat will not give pause / For your love, nor your loss, nor any cause."), the rather stark meaning is moved to the end of the sentence by the repetition of *s* sounds in all three lines, of *a* sounds in the first line, *i* sounds in the second, and *o* sounds in the third, as well as by rhyme and rhythm, in a musicality that operates to place it in the larger context of contemplation. The poignancy of the music is that of the human reach for beauty, for love. The tight construction of the sonnet form with the octave and responding sestet distills the thought in counterpoint to the beauty of sound. Feeling is both expressed and contained by form.

The first sonnet declares the strength of the will to survive the loss of love; the second muses that the loss results in less loneliness than did the unsympathetic romance: "I shall be made lonely / By simple empty days,—never that chill / Resonant heart to strike between my arms / Again, as though distraught for distance." It would seem that the "fifteenth" is the final farewell, but why were fifteen required? Is the exaggerated number a commentary on the human fear of loneliness—applying to both men and women—or is it a recognition of woman's penchant for putting up with unsatisfactory relationships rather than to be "alone" in the world? The attempt at lightness of mood in the title appears to be a nervous gesture to gain acceptance of a stance felt to be defiant.

The same defiance is manifested in "Sonnet" in imagery of bondage and ensnarement of the persona's thought. The relationship to the lover is represented as a threat in terms of elemental dangers—hot, cold, storm, wind, thundering cloud. The mind, the sense of self, fights for existence with no indication of a possibility of coexistence with a sexual relationship. Love is a "bitter spell." The only alternative for the mind to submission is to "be thrown / Straight to its freedom in the thunderous cloud." The dichotomy of selfhood and love is such that the mind is "desperate," "maddened and proud." Surely such adjectives describe a state of strong feeling, but the sonnet form serves to objectify the emotion and to move it beyond the purely personal.

Historical Meaning in Form

By using form to place a personal reflection in historical perspective, a later poem becomes a comment on modern introspection rather than on individual feeling. "Come Sleep . . .," by the allusion of the title to a lyric by John Fletcher, considers the contrast between the older view of psychology and the modern one.[25] Fletcher's poem beckons sleep as a pleasure:

> Come, Sleep, and with thy sweet deceiving,
> Lock me in delight awhile;
> Let some pleasing dreams beguile
> All my fancies;

Bogan's poem finds dreams not always pleasing. Invoking clear, strong images of genetic patterns of appearance and behavior in plants and animals, patterns designed to provide survival for the species often at the expense of other species, she wonders:

> Do the shadows of these forms and appetites
> Repeat, when these lives give over,
> In sleep, the role of the selfish devourer,
> The selfless lover?
>
> Surely, whispers in the glassy corridor
> Never trouble their dream.
> Never, for them, the dark turreted house reflects itself
> In the depthless stream.
>
> (108)

In Fletcher's poem, sleep is a "sweet deceiving," but in Bogan's poem, sleep is a disturbing confrontation. By the bringing to mind of Fletcher's seventeenth-century lyric with its convention of light-heartedness and its pleasing and musical language and rhythm, the general rhythm of a lullaby, Bogan's poem becomes the more searching and serious.

Her use of lyrical stanzas with second and fourth lines rhyming, or slant rhyming, involves the intellectual content of the poem with the subjective response to rhythm and sound. The appeal is to both the conscious and unconscious, and the imagery is of both: the images of the conscious of the first two stanzas and the images of the unconscious in the last two ("whispers in the glassy corridor" is especially wonderful in combining sound, imagery, and meaning). The tone is one of unhappy questioning rather than of being "contented with a thought / Through an idle fancy wrought." Her poem wonders about the human state that, by implication, is ruled by the same "forms and appetites" as the rest of nature, but aspires to more and, therefore, suffers. What is the place of the human conscience, or consciousness, in this design? Why, in this rapacious universe, is there human concern for the "selfish" or "selfless"? What is the nature of the haunting pains in the back of the mind that trouble sleep? Only by implication, by indirect reference to human experience, is the poem focused on the human lot, let alone on personal experience. Fletcher's easy self-concern is not available to her; therefore, the objective, generalized statement based on her own unquiet feelings is a response to his poem.

Conclusion

There is a poem written late in Bogan's life that I believe epitomizes the essential function of form in her poetry. The poem is "Lit-

tle Lobelia's Song," and the manuscript at Amherst College contains
the note, "an autonomous complex":

>I was once a part
>Of your blood and bone.
>Now no longer—
>I'm alone, I'm alone.
>
>Each day, at dawn,
>I come out of your sleep;
>I can't get back.
>I weep, I weep.
>
>Not lost but abandoned,
>Left behind;
>This is my hand
>Upon your mind.
>
>I know nothing.
>I can barely speak.
>But these are my tears
>Upon your cheek.
>
>You look at your face
>In the looking glass.
>This is the face
>My likeness has.
>
>Give me back your sleep
>Until you die,
>Else I weep, weep,
>Else I cry, cry.
>
>(132–33)

In the case of this poem, the term *song* does not indicate lightness of
mood but simple, rhythmic repetitiveness as basic as a heartbeat and
as autonomous. The vocabulary is simple, too, but the meaning is
insistently, seriously complicated: "I know nothing. / I can barely
speak. / But these are my tears / Upon your cheek." An autonomous
psychological complex is elemental and formal, and its meaning is
hidden behind and within its form. The meaning of the poem is inherent in its form, too, but in conjunction with the ordering consciousness that brings insight.

Louise Bogan once made the comment that highly formal poetry has always been obscure because the universe is difficult.[26] Form, in other words, is a ritualistic way of dealing with complexities that are beyond rational comprehension. In her poetry, I believe that form operates to deal with difficulties whose total nature remained obscure to her. That is to say, form parallels the complex structures of her feelings and thought.

Chapter Two
Louise Bogan and the Metaphysical Tradition

Influences

Lyric poetry that both expresses feelings and strives for understanding is in the oldest tradition of art from its beginning in religious ritual and is metaphysical in nature. The term *metaphysical,* however, as a result of Samuel Johnson's use of the term, is applied today to those poets who emphasize the intellectual aspect. Although Dryden referred first to Donne's *metaphysics,* Johnson used the term in criticizing the kind of complex poetry written by Donne. Bogan's poetry is often characterized as metaphysical, and with good reason. If we consider her criticism, her letters to other literary people, and her own poetry, her mature poetic values appear to have been determined by the metaphysical tradition as it was modified by the influence of the French symbolists. This position was not uncommon during the period when Bogan began writing. As she said in 1939:

Arthur Symons' The Symbolist Movement, and the French poets read at its suggestion, were strong influences experienced before I was twenty. The English metaphysicals (disinterred after 1912 and a literary fashion during my twenties) provided another literary pattern, and Yeats influenced my writing from 1916, when I first read Responsibilities.—The American writers to whom I return are Poe (the Tales), Thoreau, E. Dickinson and Henry James. Whitman, read at sixteen, with much enthusiasm, I do not return to. . . .[1]

As Eliot pointed out in his essay "The Metaphysical Poets," the French symbolists were in the metaphysical tradition in fusing thought and emotion. The symbolists differed from the metaphysicals, however, in being concerned with the sound, the musical effect, of words (ideas expressed emotionally), whereas the seventeenth-century metaphysical verse was often harsh as a result of emphasis on thought (emotion expressed intellectually).

Bogan's poetry has the intellectual emphasis of the seventeenth-century metaphysical poets but the musical language and the concern with the subconscious of the French symbolists. Like Donne, Bogan sees the individual in relationship to a larger design which is too complex to be directly perceived. Her poetry, like his, is concentrated and inductive—if one can use the term *inductive* to denote a process involving emotion as well as reason. The complexities of Bogan's poetry are those of the twentieth century, involving different problems of social demands and different bodies of belief or knowledge from those of Donne's seventeenth century. Bogan looks into the subconscious for truths with an awareness of modern psychology.

In searching the subconscious, the dream, for essence, Bogan resembles the French symbolists Baudelaire, Mallarmé, and Rimbaud. As it was to them, the music of language, sound, is important to Bogan, but always in conjunction with verbal meaning. However, like Mallarmé, she believed that meaning should be suggested, that truth is complex and elusive. In a letter to May Sarton in 1954, she explained the function of the symbol in suggesting meaning: "I liked Little Fugue [a poem by Sarton], unbreakable old *symbolist* that I am; a central symbol holds all together, and yet radiates. . . . This grand (in the Irish sense!) method Mallarmé passed on to us. . . ."[2]

As Bogan said, she encountered the symbolists when young, and her interest in Baudelaire, Mallarmé, and Rimbaud continued over the years. During the year 1936, she filled five or six notebooks in English and French with notes on the three poets.[3] Also during that year, upset with a translation of Baudelaire, she wrote a long letter to Morton Zabel listing her objections.[4]

Bogan's poetry is a fusing of learned techniques to her own statement and language. Sona Raiziss in *The Metaphysical Passion* (1952) emphasizes the influence of T. S. Eliot in such methods as combining colloquial and rhetorical speech when writing metaphysical verse for the twentieth century, a time like the seventeenth century of change and upheaval and therefore of tension. The problem is one of healing the "dissociation of sensibility" so that all elements of the poem are vital—form, thought, and feeling. Bogan felt that Eliot had found an effective way to deal with modern tension, and in an article written in 1950, she remarked that

it is only the human that can humanize. It is now equally as difficult to flood outer reality with emotion as it once was to discover the inner springs

of feeling and conduct. The world, already imaginatively dissolved, anato-
mized, and reconstituted, must now be *felt* through experience, and experienced through feeling. [Eliot's] *Four Quartets,* [Rilke's] the *Duino Elegies,*
and Apollinaire's songs and contemplations have already opened the way.[5]

Form and Feeling

To feel through experience and experience through feeling, the
poet must be in touch with the subconscious but always as apprehended by the conscious. This is what she said in an explanatory leaflet written to accompany a poem printed in folio, "July Dawn":

The lyric gift—the talent for writing lyric poetry—has been recognized,
since antiquity, as chancy and unreliable. The symbol of the Muse once represented the unknowable process by which emotion is translated into a pattern of words. The emotion must be strong enough not only to produce the
initial creative impulse, but to prefigure, in part, the structure of the poem
as a whole. Not everything is "given," but enough of the design should
come through to determine the poem's shape, direction and speed. The rest
must be filled in by the conscious mind, which, ideally, knows all the artful
devices of language.

She enlarged upon the chanciness of inspiration and the pain of the
intervals between inspirations with which a lyric poet must contend.
The only hope is to remain open and sincere, she said, and to avoid
mere self-imitation. Bogan felt it "insincere" to deal with "small
emotions" in poetry; the mind must censor the feeling. Given the
proper feeling, the feeling shapes the form because form is a matter
of beat and, like the beat of the heart or the rhythm of breathing—
or rather the contrapuntal effect of the two working together—is a
natural element of the human constitution. In other words, form is
a means to an end, and that end is to transform the emotion of the
poet into one experienced by the reader or hearer.
    In this discussion of form Bogan did not include metaphor or idea,
but she did in a letter to Theodore Roethke in 1935 in which she
offered two poems by Rilke as illustration of what a poem should be:

You get a terrific patience and power of *looking,* in "the Blue Hortensia"
one, and in the other you get a magnificent single poetic concept carried
through with perfect ease, because it is thoroughly informed by passion, in
the first place. In the latter poem Rilke is terribly upset about his inability
to get away from it all—you know that without my telling you, but let me

maunder on. So he starts to write a poem, and he turns the lack of freedom into a perfectly frightful metaphor: he is unable to see any distance, any horizon (lovely word!), and he is so unable to see any that he feels himself *inside* a mountain, like a vein of ore. Everything is nearness, and all the nearness stone. Magnificent. And then what happens? Well, he can't stand it, so he turns to someone for help, and he drags the person into the metaphor. *I* am not adept at pain, he says, but if *you* are, make yourself heavy (isn't that *schwer* wonderful?) and break in, so that your whole hand may fall upon me and I on you with my whole cry. . . . Now, a poem like that cannot be written by technique alone. It is carved out of agony, just as a statue is carved out of marble.

Metaphor, then, is organic form also because it is shaped by feeling to express the otherwise inexpressible. What she called the "power of *looking*" (the flooding of "outer reality with emotions") is illustrated in the discussion of "The Blue Hortensia":

"The Blue Hortensia" plumbs blue hortensia to their depths. Here all sorts of comparisons are brought in, to aid the plumbing process. The color of the flowers is the color of old writing paper, faded into yellow and violet and gray, and it is like a child's many-times-washed apron—and by the time the reader gets to that, he is in a state of collapse, for Rilke has re-created the color in such a moving way that it's as though something new had been created in the universe.[6]

This makes it plain that, to Bogan, idea is carried by metaphor and imagery, and imagery must be concrete. The reader's experience should be direct with as little interference from the poet as possible. In a letter to Rolfe Humphries in 1935, she expressed dissatisfaction with her poem "Roman Fountain" because it did not have this kind of objectivity: "To Hell with that poem. It's minor, all save the first stanza. It doesn't do it. It should be all fountain, and no Louise looking at it."[7]

Concreteness and Sincerity

Whenever Bogan criticized her own poetry it was usually on the basis of its lacking either concreteness of image or sincerity of feeling ("sincerity" demanding a certain importance, or largeness, of feeling, remember). She did not want some early poems reprinted because she had come to see them as "mawkish" ("Song," discussed in chapter 1, is one of these). As she explained to John Hall Wheelock, editor of her volume *Poems and New Poems* (1941), when they were deciding upon poems: "It isn't that I'm turning on my early self. But the girl of 23 and 24, who wrote most of these early poems, was so seldom mawkish, that I want her not to be mawkish at all."[8] Another poem, "The Flume," after being published first in *The Measure* in June 1925, then collected in *Dark Summer,* was not reprinted because she was not sure that it was "true":

I have never been quite sure about "The Flume." It came from the right place, and I worked hard on it, and it has some nice moments—the hot stove and the no-sound of water—which were actually observed and lived with, at one period of my life. Perhaps I have the feeling that one doesn't get out of that kind of obsession so easily—the "facts" are false, at the end.[9]

In her attempt to realize concreteness and sincerity, Bogan tended to concentrate her meaning by editing to shorten, resulting in increased tension. This practice is best illustrated by considering the evolution of one poem from the original version enclosed in a letter to Edmund Wilson to its final form as published. The original is:

Lines Written After Detecting in Myself a Yearning Toward the Large, Wise, Calm, Richly Resigned, Benignant Act Put on by a Great Many People After Having Passed the Age of Thirty-Five.

For every great soul who died in his house and his wisdom
Several did otherwise.
God, keep me from the fat heart that looks vaingloriously toward peace
    and maturity;
Protect me not from lies.
In Thy infinite certitude, tenderness and mercy
Allow me to be sick and well,
So that I may never tread with swollen foot the calm and obscene
    intentions
That pave hell.
Shakespeare, Milton, Matthew Arnold died in their beds,
Dante above the stranger's stair.
They were not absolved from either the courage or the cowardice
With which they bore what they had to bear.
Swift died blind, deaf and mad;
Socrates died in his cell;
Baudelaire died in his drool;
Proving no rule.[10]

and the finished poem became

To an Artist, to Take Heart

Slipping in blood, by his own hand, through pride,
Hamlet, Othello, Coriolanus fall.
Upon his bed, however, Shakespeare died,
Having endured them all.

(104)

Bogan's tendency to concentration can at times cause obscurity, if not enough is given (a fault critics have found with some other metaphysical poets). More often, though, Bogan uses a controlling image effectively, as in "Winter Swan," where the swan contains the enigma of mutability. After the first five lines which express the speaker's anguish at the passing of youth in terms of imagery of winter, the swan is addressed: "But speak, you proud! / Where lies the leaf-caught world once thought abiding, / Now but a dry disarray and artifice?" This poem also affords an example of Bogan's use of synaesthesia, the simultaneous appeal to several senses, a symbolist influence, in the clause "the live blood shouts aloud." The conflicting elements of the life force and death are summed up in the final image of the swan with the perfect verb *drifts* (perfect because it both expresses the state of the life force in the poem and is the customary mode of movement of the swan) and "the long throat bent back, and the eyes in hiding."[11]

"The Alchemist" is another poem that illustrates both the metaphysical qualities of Bogan's work and the symbolist quality of musical language characteristic of her.[12] In two stanzas of mostly tetrameter couplets, of assonance and consonance, that create a lyrical movement of the lines that appeals to the senses, the harshness of the thought is the more grim ("I burned my life, that I might find / A passion wholly of the mind"). The alchemist is burning the demands of physical existence to distill a life of the mind free from grief as the medieval alchemists tried to distill gold from baser metals. Like them, the poet fails: "I had found unmysterious flesh— / Not the mind's avid substance—still / Passionate beyond the will." That the conceit is developed in images of destruction—"burned," "divorced," "broke," "flawed," "charred"—makes the final endurance of feeling the more imperious. In addition to other meanings in the poem, the frame of reference of the metaphysical poet is expressed here, it seems to me, in the first two lines.

This is the frame of reference that Bogan retained, and she remained true to her kind of condensed lyric even though the movement of American poetry was in another direction after the 1930s. By her own account:

The whole lyrical school, in fact, now began to suffer an eclipse. It was a school which could too easily be enfeebled by the functioning of feeble gifts within it. Its virtues of simple directness, if not kept absolutely clear, faded into inanity. Its high tension was difficult to sustain. When unmixed with new hardness and vigor, its forms dropped into limpness or its emotion receded into bathos. Female lyric grief soon came in for some ridicule, and not a little contempt. In 1937, a member of the Poets Session of the League of American Writers decided that "the lyric is dead." His remark met with little skepticism. [13]

The lyric was not dead for her, though. She remained interested in newer modes of writing, reviewed them, and served on prize committees for young poets; but she held fast to her own values. While recognizing the contribution of experimentalists in an article written in 1957, "Experimentalists of a New Generation," she concluded that

after experiencing the poems of Baudelaire, Mallarmé, Hopkins, Valéry, Pound, Eliot, and Auden, the sensibilities of the contemporary reader demand some subtlety, some actual largeness of concept, some interesting effects of language, and some true wit. Originality, now as always, depends upon individual powers of insight, individual intensity, and an individual way with words. Loud shouts, extreme stances, exhibitionism of one kind or another are not the means the imagination takes to let the light through. [14]

The Fear of "Small" Emotions

Her poetry, for the most part, stands up to her own criteria. She was consistent in her criticism and her practice. Do her criteria have validity for poetry today? This is the question that remains. I believe that her metaphysical mode is certainly valid for today; its inherent tension can be very expressive of the complexity of contemporary life. And music and wit are still welcome—wit in the sense both of educated intelligence and of humor. However, the necessity for an emotion not to be "small" is hampering to Bogan, I feel, because it causes her, on occasion, by the assumption of a certain loftiness, to

disguise a feeling that she finds inadequate. One such occasion is the
poem "Zone":

> We have struck the regions wherein we are keel or reef.
> The wind breaks over us,
> And against high sharp angles almost splits into words,
> And these are of fear or grief.
>
> Like a ship, we have struck expected latitudes
> Of the universe, in March.
> Through one short segment's arch
> Of the zodiac's round
> We pass,
> Thinking: Now we hear
> What we heard last year,
> And bear the wind's rude touch
> And its ugly sound
> Equally with so much
> We have learned how to bear.
>
> (109)

She chose this poem as a favorite with the explanation:

"Zone was written in the later 30's in a transitional period both of my outer
circumstances and my central beliefs. It is, therefore, a poem which derives
directly from emotional crisis, as, I feel, a lyric must. And I think that the
poem's imagery manages to express, in concrete terms (the concrete terms
which poetry demands) some reflection of those relentless universal laws, under which we live—which we must not only accept, but in some manner,
forgive—as well as the fact of the human courage and faith necessary to that
acceptance. [15]

The poem, to me, is not about courage but about "fear or grief," and
the last two lines seem tacked on. Without them, the poem expresses
endurance—less noble, perhaps, than courage and faith.

Then there are the early poems that she felt to be mawkish which
were really not that at all but rather were attempting to express emotions that she did not respect. Perhaps Bogan would have saved more
of her work, and even written more, if she had had a less exclusive
attitude toward feeling. But then, conflict between conscious and unconscious is part of the tension of her poetry and a part that speaks
to contemporary society.

Relationship to Metaphysical Tradition

The combined influences of symbolism and the English metaphysicals may account for some seeming oppositions in Bogan's poetry. While her view of the lyric as requiring "a high tension," "hardness and vigor," and "simple directness" (by which I believe she means common and exact speech) suggests the metaphysicals, her romantic stress on individual intensity and powers is contradictory to the metaphysicals, who saw themselves more often in relation to their society, but in accord with the symbolists. Her metaphors often deal with nature or with the human body, sometimes with music, and are usually of the complexity of the metaphysicals rather than of the luxuriantly sensual of the symbolists. I have already mentioned the use of synaesthesia and the feeling for musical sound in Bogan's poetry as symbolist characteristics. Unlike Herbert, Donne, and Vaughn, she is not concerned with formal religious problems. She is, however, concerned with whatever forces she feels order the universe.

Although her statements about a poet's "seeing" objects with feeling until something new is created sound like Wallace Stevens, who was also influenced by the symbolists, she differs from him in believing in an outside ordering force, whereas Stevens believed that the poet must create his own order. An even greater difference is that her poetry is more intense, more concerned with human passion, whereas Stevens's poetry is cooler in feeling and less directly concerned with relations between people, although both try to distance themselves from their poetry.

The basic quality that Bogan has in common with metaphysical poets of any time or temperament is a driving curiosity about essence, certainly a timeless human concern. As Joseph E. Duncan has said: "Metaphysical poetry has thrived on a search for cosmological and psychological integration. Though there has been some reaction against it, as the embodiment of this quest it will live until the search is ended or the goal is appreciably changed."[16]

Chapter Three
Early Poems

Early Romanticism

Among the Bogan papers at Amherst College I found a clipping of a poem that Ruth Limmer tells me was published in the Girls' Latin School publication, *Jabberwock,* during the time Bogan attended the school, probably when she was about sixteen. It is titled "A Night in Summer" and signed "Louise M. Bogan." It is a sonnet describing the sound of the breaking sea at night. With an *abba abba cde ced* rhyme scheme in iambic pentameter, the poem illustrates both Bogan's early facility with traditional form and her ear for subtle variations of beat and aural line length. Even though the repetition of the word *sad* reveals the writer's immaturity, the alliteration of the *s* sounds effectively brings to mind the sound of the quiet surf. The meaning of the poem in like fashion contains both the child's sense of romance and an underlying implication of a theme that is to dominate Bogan's adult poetry, the feeling that life is cyclic and patterned, subordinating the individual or particular. The "unrest," "sad memory, / Of cadences that come and swiftly flee," "longingly," "sighing," "fading each in each" suggest the poignancy of beginning and end, while the "stars that bend to see" suggest the eternal. I believe that Bogan's later work shows how ingrained in her was this view of the universe.

The other poems belong to a year when Bogan was attending Boston University. Still under the influence of her reading, especially the romantics, and still childishly idealistic, Bogan nevertheless was going in her own direction and seeking her own answers. Both poems were published in the Boston University *Beacon* when Bogan was eighteen years old.[1] The first, "A Carol," which appeared in the Christmas issue in 1915, is the simplest and employs the form of a song, a form that was to be used with variations throughout her life. The archaic language, the simplicity of tone and theme suggesting an old English carol are romantic in effect, but there are also elements that are characteristic of later Bogan poetry. The feeling for spring

23

and morning as propitious times and winter and night as foreboding times is here, although the season, time, and circumstance are brightened by God's favor. Such optimistic affirmation of religious hope was not to remain in her work, however.

The other poem, "The Betrothal of King Cophetua," was published in April 1916 and also harks back to an earlier English form, a medieval ballad that appears in one form in Percy's *Reliques* as "King Cophetua and the Beggarmaid." I believe, though, that Bogan was inspired to write her poem by Tennyson's "The Beggar Maid" which is based on the old ballad but differs from it, although she had probably read both poems.[2] Like Tennyson's poem, her version is much shorter than the old ballad, omits Cupid and his dart as the cause of the king's infatuation, and presents the maid as coming before the king rather than having the king go among the beggars at the palace gate to find her. In other words, both Bogan and Tennyson wrote their poems in the spirit of nineteenth-century romanticism rather than medieval romance. But Bogan's poem differs from Tennyson's poem as well in a significant way. In Tennyson's poem the king is attracted to the beggar maid because her beauty overcomes the difference in social status. It is a measure of her beauty that such a gap is bridged and with the approval of the lords at court. Mention of her "lovesome mien" and "sweet" face are the only hints of her personality or character, and there are no hints of the nature of the king's character except for his determination ("Cophetua sware a royal oath") to have this rare beauty for his queen. The language of the poem is musical, contributing to the aspect of pleasant fantasy, and the simile "As shines the moon in clouded skies, / She in her poor attire was seen," contains both the contrast of brightness and darkness in the relative social positions and the idea of the unattainable. There is the traditional suggestion of the feminine in the moon as symbol, too, of course. Overall, the poem is a romantic dream, a fairy tale of societal obstacles overcome:

The Beggar Maid

Her arms across her breast she laid;
    She was more fair than words can say;
Barefooted came the beggar maid
    Before the king Cophetua.
In robe and crown the king stept down,
    To meet and greet her on her way;
"It is no wonder," said the lords,

"She is more beautiful than day."
As shines the moon in clouded skies,
    She in her poor attire was seen;
One praised her ankles, one her eyes,
    One her dark hair and lovesome mien.
So sweet a face, such angel grace,
    In all that land had never been.
Cophetua sware a royal oath:
    "This beggar maid shall be my queen!"

Bogan's version is a romantic story, too, with romanticized language
and exotic detail, but there is an attempt to reconcile romance with
reality by creating psychological motivation for both the king's infatuation and the maid's acceptance of his proposal of marriage—
motivation more personal than that of beauty or rank. Human complexity is somewhat taken into consideration, and the rhythm of the
poem reflects it in a variation in fast and slow movement and in beat,
as well as variation in the rhyme scheme. The king is drawn to the
maid not because she is beautiful (there is no description of her as
beautiful) but because she summons up "old dreams / His youth
knew." She is drawn to him not by wealth and position but by
love—a youthful, fanciful concept of love, to be sure, but a concept
that nevertheless aspires to real affection. The "fairy tale" comes to
represent not merely fantasy but youthful idealism. As in "A Carol,"
the tone is optimistic:

The Betrothal of King Cophetua

When they had brought her at the king's behest,
The courtyard dusk fell cool to her forehead's heat,
She silent stood, the sun on her bruised feet.
The evening shadow lay against her breast.

            "Your name?" he asked.
            "I have not any name."
Her round voice held the sound of windless streams
Fringed to the bank with grasses—of old dreams

His youth knew. His words broke, and he was mute,
Then asked again "You come from out what land?"
            "I have forgotten."
            Under trees of fruit
He had seen her first as they bowed in the ripening year,

Fragrant her lips with fruit, and stained her hand.
He said "Come nearer," and she came more near.

A casket then he gave to her like flame
Beneath the lid, like flame into the dark
The jewels sprawled and looped and shot their spark
Star-wise: periodot, beryl, winy sard
And icy straps of diamond.
                                        Above,
Beyond where to the sky the roof cut hard
Called, notes like heavy water to a wave
Were falling, and with pain her heart knew love.
The box crashed, the heaped gems spilled to the pave.

Blindly, through the dark, to his side she came,
Her feet seemed shod with rain so swift they were.
Like wings on her forehead folded lay her hair,
And she was wild and sweet.
                                        "I am a king,"
He said, "But if I give you jewels, lands,
And you spurn all, I have no other thing,
No more to give, if it be not love you seek . . ."
Leaning, he took her face between his hands;
She turned her eyes to him, and did not speak.

Breakdown of Early Idealism

Bogan as a mature poet was not to write romantic, optimistic poetry; and it is for this very reason that it is helpful to read poems of
her adolescence. They aid in understanding the "bitterness which
comes with a breakdown of early idealism" that she struggled against
later in her work and in herself. Many years later, in a letter to May
Sarton in which she was commenting upon a poem of Sarton's, she
remarked: "Can we use the word *beloved*? Why not, really; but that
Romantic vocabulary comes v. [very] hard, to me, having spent years
getting away from it—since William Morris and Dante Gabriel R.
were the people I imitated, during my apprenticeship."[3] The romantic vocabulary vanished, but the imagery of shadow and sunlight,
concern with the time of day and with season, and the imagery of
streams, waves, grasses, and fruit in conjunction with romantic love
suggesting a universal cycle larger than human experience were to be
characteristic.

By the end of the following year, 1917, the romantic idealism was over; and two poems printed in the December issue of *Others,* a little magazine, reflect that fact. An unhappy marriage appears to have precipitated the disillusionment. Bogan had married Curt Alexander, an army man, in September 1916 and followed him to the Panama Canal Zone. Her daughter Mathilde (Maidie) was born there in 1917. The marriage didn't last long, and the couple separated before Alexander's death in 1920. The two poems, "Betrothed" and "The Young Wife," appeared on opposite pages of the magazine.[4] Printed just a year and eight months after "The Betrothal of King Cophetua," they contain many of the same images that appear in the earlier poem as a reassessment of romantic expectation is made. In "Betrothed" the movement of the lines in free verse is slower as though the words were more considered, and the romantic concepts are held up for rational analysis. The question "What have I thought of love?" is answered in terms of "beauty and sorrow," "lost delights," and "splendor / As a wind out of old time," followed by the reflection on these former feelings of the concluding three lines: "But there is only the evening here, / And the sound of willows / Now and again dipping their long oval leaves in the water." This poem was to be reprinted in Bogan's first volume of poetry, *Body of This Death,* and to be included in her final volume, *The Blue Estuaries;* therefore, it is a poem she still liked in maturity.

The other poem, "The Young Wife," was never reprinted. It is not hard to see why Bogan would reject this poem later on because it is a rambling eight stanzas long in two parts and is somewhat immature in thought. However, parts of the poem are interesting because they contain elements of the imagery and ideas in "King Cophetua" but in changing context. The first verse seems a direct response to the earlier poem with the lines "I do not believe in this first happiness. / But one day I shall know that love is not a fruited bough / Low bending to the hand." Rather than in images of nature's bounty freely offered, love is defined in images of nature's inexorable, impersonal force, as the wind, and as the spring tree whose roots are "throbbing in darkness." The young wife, no matter how beautiful, cannot be "as beautiful as all beautiful women." Again there is the imagery of the voice as the sound of water, but the music has lost its magic. Love is an unrealizable hope engendered by an implacable life force and the societal restrictions and romantic conventions that cause the young to expect the impossible. Disillusionment with the unique-

ness or permanence of romantic love has taken place; and Bogan's poetry, although it becomes more philosophical and objective, is never
to reflect any other view.

Besides disillusionment, "The Young Wife" contains a theme of
distrust and jealousy—probably another reason Bogan did not reprint
it. As will be discussed further on, disturbing early family experiences seem to have haunted Bogan all her life and interfered with her
happiness and peace of mind. Many of her poems reflect her effort to
resolve these emotional problems and to understand the meaning of
human relationships.

Another poem in free verse, also uncollected with later poems, is
worthy of being collected, I believe. Called "Survival," it was published in the *Measure* in November 1921 (no. 9, p. 5). The imagery
is again of nature and the seasons, but also of the failure of time to
make a wanted change. The tone is level and cool despite the vivid
evocation of color and of the threatening inexorability of winter:

> I hoped that you would die out from me
> With the year.
> Between you and my heart I thrust
> The glittering seasons.
>
> I denied you with late summer,
> Watching the green-white hydrangea change
> To petalled balls of thin and ashen blue,
> And nasturtiums, hot orange on stems like ice or glass
> Shriveling by round leaves.
>
> I went on to autumn
> Without you,
> Seeing hills burdened by trees colored unevenly:
> Applered, pearyellow,
> And leaves falling in ravines, through bitter smoke,
> Falling indirectly,
> A long waver and turn.
> Those evenings came
> High and shining over rivers like quicksilver;
> And latest autumn:
> The underbrush sienna, cut, twisted, carved,
> Red berries shaken through it like beads
> Scattered in barbaric hair.

> Nothing moves in the fields that once had the grass.
> To look upon the fields
> Is like silence laid upon the eyes.
> The house is shut sternly
> From limitless radiance outside
> In these days of afternoon stars.
>
> The year dies out.
> Who are you to be stronger than the year?
> I have you like long cold sunshine in an empty room,
> Through and beyond black thaws that rot the snow.

The movement from color, warmth, and life to barrenness, coldness, and darkness parallels the theme of emotional loss with only three modifiers—"*bitter* smoke," "*barbaric* hair," and "shut *sternly*"—hinting at their oneness. The promise of nature is indifferent to the single and survives beyond the seasonal end ("Who are you to be stronger than the year?"). I wonder that Bogan discarded a poem that so effectively manifests her perception of life as an ordering beyond the aspiring reach of the individual.

The temporality of love, equated with the temporality of the seasons, in the face of a continuing life force is also the theme of a group of five poems published in *Poetry* magazine in August 1922 under the title "Beginning and End." The poems seem to sum up Bogan's progress from early romanticism and unwise marriage to a bleak acceptance of disappointment: "Elders" voices the empty promise of fulfillment; "Resolve" employs the metaphor of a shield for the emotional defense against hurt; "Knowledge" is a cynical comment on human passion; "Leave-taking" is a sad attempt to be philosophical about a painful separation; and "To a Dead Lover" is a reflection on the death of love as well as on the death of the lover and concludes:

> That I may not remember
> Does not matter.
> I shall not be with you again.
> What we knew, even now
> Must scatter
> And be ruined, and blow
> Like dust in the rain.
>
> You have been dead a long season
> And have less than desire

> Who were lover with lover;
> And I have life—that old reason
> To wait for what comes,
> To leave what is over.[5]

Of this group of five poems, only "Knowledge" was reprinted in later collections. Its more objective tone was to be the characteristic tone of Bogan's mature poetry. The form of "Knowledge," conventional and rhymed, is instructive, too, of the direction that Bogan's poetry was to take in that, as she removed what she considered the purely personal, she relied upon form to carry the emotional weight.

Development of a Mature Voice

In these poems of Bogan's early twenties, she was struggling with a changing life view and experimenting with style in an effort to write her own poetry. Early influences and ways of feeling were in tension with current ones to produce a mixture of romanticism and twentieth-century disenchantment, of traditional forms and free verse. The influence of the nineteenth-century Christina Rossetti, for instance, is suggested in "To a Dead Lover" with its reverberation of Rossetti's "Song" ("When I am dead, my dearest, / Sing no sad songs for me") that has as conclusion "Haply I may remember, / And haply may forget." During the same period, suggesting the influence of the disillusioned twenties, Bogan was also writing a light, cynical little verse such as "Pyro-technics" which appeared in the May 1923 *Liberator*.[6] It is a four-line, *carpe diem* admonition ending "Burn, bridges, burn!"

But in "Trio," another such poem, which appeared in the June 1923 *Measure* (no. 28, p. 12), bitterness underlies the flippancy. The meaning is that joy is doomed by time—and by people ("Savor the perishing minute / By the grave that you dug, my dears, / Even though I'm not in it"). In the same issue and on the same page, another poem by Bogan, "The Stones," deals with the difficulty of love to surmount old scars of the psyche with the metaphor of stones as cold, hard, and bruising to hands that reach out. It is uneven in both expression and rhythm. None of the three represents Bogan's best work. They seem to have been experiments in finding the proper voice and tone, and she chose to drop them from later collections.

Overall, however, Bogan was developing rapidly as a poet, and in September 1923 her first volume of poetry, *Body of This Death,* was published. The intensity of feeling and underlying seriousness of thought predominantly characteristic of Bogan from childhood on were finding unified expression in poems where thought, feeling, and form were one.

Chapter Four
Body of This Death

When *Body of This Death* was published, opposite the title page was the quotation: "Who shall deliver me from the body of this death?"[1] It is from Paul's Epistle to the Romans, of course; and the Douai Bible, the Bible with which Louise Bogan as a Catholic child was probably the most familiar, contains this version of 7:23–24:

> But I see another law in my members, fighting against the law of my mind, and captivating me in the law of sin, that is in my members.
> Unhappy man that I am, who shall deliver me from the body of this death?

In addition to this direct source of Bogan's quotation, I think an indirect reference found in Symons's *The Symbolist Movement in Literature* should be considered to furnish a possibly modifying context, for Bogan was influenced very early by Symons. In his discussion of Mallarmé, Symons says:

> It is the distinction of Mallarmé to have aspired after an impossible liberation of the soul of literature from what is fretting and constraining in "the body of that death," which is the mere literature of words. Words, he has realized, are of value only as a notation of the free breath of the spirit; words, therefore, must be employed with an extreme care, in their choice and adjustment, in setting them to reflect and chime upon one another; yet least of all for their own sake, for what they can never, except by suggestion, express. . . . The word, chosen as he chooses it, is for him a liberating principle, by which the spirit is extracted from matter; takes form, perhaps assumes immortality.[2]

The "body of this death" becomes the weight of words on the artist's aspiration to expression as well as Paul's weight of sin on the soul's aspiration to goodness. In both cases, there is the weight of physical limitation on the mind or spirit.

The Goal of Objectivity

Bogan is concerned in this volume to move beyond both her younger romanticism and what she felt to be the purely personal—to find an objective poetic meaning. Many of the poems had previously appeared in print (acknowledgments are given to the *New Republic,* the *Measure, Others, Poetry: A Magazine of Verse, Voices,* the *Liberator, Vanity Fair, Rhythmus,* and the *Literary Review* of the *New York Evening Post*), but, as I have said, Bogan chose to eliminate those poems no longer meeting her approval. Satire becomes preferable to romantic idealism, although bitterness rather than "mawkishness" becomes the fault of her "breakdown of early idealism."[3] She uses free verse as well as more traditional rhyme and stanza patterns, but seems to be most expressive in the tighter forms where symbol, sound, and image can raise meaning above the "body" of language.

She is concerned, too, with the human body which she sees as a part of the universal cycle of death and renewal, and its relationship to the mind and spirit which seem to demand more than existence. While never echoing Paul's concern with "sin," Bogan seeks universal patterns and implications in the human lot. Those poems that she came to see as expressing merely personal confusion and pain she continued to drop from her collections over the years. One poem included in this first volume, "The Alchemist," voices the struggle of the "mind's avid substance" to surmount the pains and limitations of "unmysterious flesh": "I had found unmysterious flesh— / Not the mind's avid substance—still / Passionate beyond the will." These last three lines compare to Paul's lines in Romans 7:25—"Therefore, I myself with the mind serve the law of God; but with the flesh, the law of sin"—in seeing the body as tyrannizing the mind, but they differ in seeing the danger as a state of meaninglessness rather than of evil. The "law of flesh" is seen as cruel rather than sinful.

Death as the Ultimate Denial

It is meaninglessness or futility in conjunction with human aspiration or need that provides the tension for the poems in this volume. Aspiration or need, even denied, is preferable to nothingness. The inevitability of death, seen as the only alternative to the pain of struggle but the ultimate denial, makes the interim struggle worthwhile by comparison. Five of the twenty-seven poems that make up

the volume express this conviction in a manner that varies from the
satiric to the serious. If these five poems are read in the order in
which they appear in the book (interrupted by only one other poem,
"The Romantic"), first is "Knowledge" reprinted from the group
"Beginning and End," followed by "Portrait" with its bitter play on
words in the last stanza:

> What she has gathered, and what lost,
> She will not find to lose again.
> She is possessed by time, who once
> Was loved by men.
>
> (11)

"My Voice Not Being Proud" employs the first person and is, if anything, more bitterly satiric in tone. After the emotional harshness of
these poems, there is the tranquility of "Statue and Birds" with the
subject literally objectified to a marble statue and all life represented
by the birds moving outside. The images are of enclosement, winter,
and devitalization to suggest the coldness of the marble, but the figure the marble forms is of human vitality, "like the arrested wind."
The statue is seen as though it were a former human who has forsaken
life and is now akin to the withered vines: "The inquietudes of the
sap and of the blood are spent." But to the observer/poet this state is
intolerable, and the positions of the outstretched hands and lifted
heel are interpreted as a desire to escape. Despite the "inquietudes"
of life, it is unbearable to be unaware of "the whistle of the birds."
The interweaving of nature and human experience in one universal
cycle is an integral part of Bogan's view. She very often translates
emotion into images of the natural world, as she does here with images of angles and sharpness and woods "raking" the sky (in the first
two stanzas describing the lifeless situation of the statue) reflecting
the "alarm" seen in the gesture of the hands. The surrounding birds,
as life, have color and motion but are not without disturbing parallels: the "quill of the fountain" in the second stanza is echoed by the
"arrowy wings" and "sharp tails" of the pheasants in the third stanza.
The fear of nothingness and the ambivalent feeling toward life are re-
solved in the last stanza where "the whistle of the birds / Fails on her
breast" suggests the desirability of life and the death of spirit and
hope as the ultimate disaster.

Bogan chose to follow "Statue and Birds," and to conclude the theme, with an ironic poem, "Epitaph for a Romantic Woman":

> She has attained the permanence
> She dreamed of, where old stones lie sunning.
> Untended stalks blow over her
> Even and swift, like young men running.
>
> Always in the heart she loved
> Others had lived,—she heard their laughter.
> She lies where none has lain before,
> Where certainly none will follow after.[4]

She later dropped this from her collections—possibly because of its theme of jealousy. However, there is a remarkable conjunction of theme (inconstancy of lovers) and image of nature in the simile describing the grave of the "romantic woman": "Untended stalks blow over her / Even and swift, like young men running." Carelessness seen in both nature and men is contained in the figure which is also an accurate description of a neglected grave.

The Price of Striving

Another poem in *Body of This Death* which Bogan did not later reprint is very different in form and mood, but also depends upon natural imagery to carry the emotional burden. In fact, only one line of the sonnet refers directly to human beings. As opposed to the naturalness of the "untended stalks," though, the imagery is highly fantastic and as if seen in a dream, a vision of the subconscious rather than the conscious. Titled "Decoration," the poem is an exotic picture of tropical lushness of which a macaw is the symbol. The extremes of natural beauty seem brutal: "claw-like leaves clutch light till it has bled." In this setting, "A gillyflower spans its little height / And lovers with their mouths press out their grief," as though both the gillyflower and the lovers are at the mercy of such extravagant power. The color, heat, and violence of the imagery of the octave is in conjunction with a description of disappointed high expectation. The macaw "preens upon a branch outspread / With jewelry of seed" but is "deaf and mute" and has the "frustrate look of cheated kings." The sestet presents the colorlessness and limitations

of actuality along with the hope (the lovers, like the gillyflower, per-
severe), but a hint of reconciliation is found in the "prismatic" fan of
the macaw against "a sky breath-white," as though life (breath) contained all the colors. But nature also contains death which frustrates
life ("A crystal tree lets fall a crystal leaf") and is not health-white
but of a harder, colder colorlessness.

Obscurity is a fault in "Decoration," and a mixture of moods of
violence and peace illustrated by the concluding line of the octave and
the beginning line of the sestet ("He has the frustrate look of cheated
kings. / And all the simple evening passes by") is not really absolved
by the ending. Perhaps the title is ironic and suggests the futility of
expectation. Still, despite its seeming lack of unity, I believe the
poem is worthy of reprinting for its vivid imagery and musical
language.

"A Tale," discussed earlier, also involves the difficulties of aspiration and is also distanced in metaphor and image. While more complex in meaning and a better integrated poem than "Decoration," it
too employs exotic nature imagery of heat and violence in conjunction
with that of quietness. However, in this poem it is clearly stated that
the quester can coexist with opposing forces: "But he will find that
nothing dares / To be enduring, *save* where. . . ."

"Last Hill in a Vista" is even clearer in its statement that the price
of striving is not too much to pay to escape "stiff walls" and "the
wooden town," safe though they are. Here the hazy, far-off hills signify the nature of hope, the "more fragile boundary" of the imagination, but they are seen from "sparse and sodden pastures" with only
"weeds in ditches" and "some cold stranger" for companionship in
contrast to the alternate "riches" and "comforts" of the town. To
want other than that which society wants is to be lonely, the poem
seems to say, but is worth it. Again, the imagery of nature is metaphor for the human condition: the protagonist is a "weed," too, and
as alive. Every word of this poem contributes on multiple levels of
meaning—by sound, pace, and imagery, and by literal as well as
metaphoric sense—to the unity of the theme. It has the concentration
that Bogan often achieves in seemingly simple poems.

"Medusa"

A very concentrated poem, "Medusa" is, I believe, central in Bogan's work. A poem of the subconscious, as Bogan believed the best
lyrics to be, it deals with an area of her subconscious that exerted a

powerful and lifelong effect upon her. Sister Angela sees the symbol of the Medusa as a controlling image in Bogan's poetry:

> In her poetry Louise Bogan can be found to subscribe to a basic tragic view of life, and she offers the Medusa as symbolically containing within itself the chief sources of life's tragedies. Introduced by the poem "Medusa," in her first book *Body of This Death,* published in 1923, the Gorgon can be found to be the dominating image in her work, containing within its multiple meanings all the major themes which preoccupy her.[5]

Further on, she says of Bogan's work: "She points to the basic source of her own tragic view of life: the accepted social order which not only does not support, but even denies, one's selfhood and individuality."[6]

The social order as a "body of this death" from which selfhood and creativity must be delivered is certainly a central view in Bogan's work. But I believe that within that general view, the poem "Medusa" is a personal, specific expression of constraining, even paralyzing forces. It seems to me that "Medusa" focuses upon Bogan's childhood anxieties, especially her conflicting feelings toward her mother which some of her writings suggest were those of admiration and love in conjunction with resentment and fear. She particularly resented her mother's lack of openness. Bogan's words to May Sarton make evident the power of Bogan's feelings toward her mother of which she said, as noted earlier, "The most poignant and enduring things in the relationship are in my poetry. The rest exhausted me forever." Her prose writings, however, offer glimpses of the nature of the feelings.

Two pieces of her writing are especially instructive. One, the autobiographical "Journey Around My Room," reflects upon the events in her past that brought her to be where she is at the particular time of writing.[7] As her eyes roam around her room, they rest on objects that bring back crucial events of her past in imagery that recurs in a more objective context in her poetry. Early fears of separation, of the mill flume, of failure of courage are expressed explicitly. She ponders the step that started her on her way and decides that it was her taking the train to Boston in 1909 (when she was eleven years old):

I am going away. I shan't ever see again old Leonard, or Shattuck's store, or the hydrangea bushes in front of Forrest Scott's house that in autumn spilled dusty-blue petals over the grass, or the mill dam, or the mill, or the swing in Gardners' yard, or the maple tree in my own, or the hedge of arbor vitae around the Congregationalist church.

The memory ends with an image of the steam of the engine obscuring her view as she boards the train: "The steam shrieks out of the engine and smoke trails out, into the clear morning, from the smokestack, blotting out the willows and the mill dam. The conductor lifts me up to the step." The overwhelming nature of the image becomes apparent in the conclusion of the piece when, after describing the objects in the "journey" around her room, she says that it is at this point of completing the reverie that she has a recurring dream:

I am set upon by sleep, and hear the rush of water, and hear the mill dam, fuming with water that weighs itself into foam against the air, and see the rapids at its foot that I must gauge and dare and swim. Give over, says this treacherous element, the fear and distress in your breast; and I pretend courage and brave it at last, among rocks along the bank, and plunge into the wave that mounts like glass to the level of my eye. O death, O fear! The universe swings up against my sight, the universe fallen into and bearing with the mill stream. I must in a moment die, but for a moment I breathe, upheld, and see all weight, all force, all water, compacted into the glassy wave, veined, marbled with foam, this moment caught raining over me. And into the wave sinks the armoire, the green bureau, the lamps, the shells from the beach in Maine. All these objects, provisional at best, now equally lost, rock down to translucent depths below fear, an Atlantis in little, under the mill stream (last seen through the steam from the Boston train in March, 1909).

The other piece that deals with Bogan's childhood feelings is a short story entitled "Dove and Serpent"[8] that Bogan referred to when describing a novel she worked on for years but never finished. The novel would be a little like "Dove and Serpent," she said in a letter to John Hall Wheelock in 1934. It would be called *Laura Dailey's Story* and would have on its title page

the remark of La Rochefoucauld:

> L'accent et le caractère du pays où
> l'on est né demeure dans l'esprit
> et dans le coeur comme dans le langage.

> [The accent and the character of the country
> where one is born reside in the spirit and
> in the heart as well as in the language.]

And I told you how the thing should be a "play of sensibility" over the mill-towns of my childhood.[9]

When one looks closely at "Dove and Serpent," one recognizes elements and people from "Journey Around My Room." There is "Mrs. Gardiner, who lived across the street," the Congregationalist church, and Old Jack Leonard. A Stella Dailey is mentioned, also, a character perhaps connected with the Laura Dailey of the projected novel. The short story deals with the disturbing impressions of childhood that remain a part of the adult psychological state. As the persona explains in the context of her childish bewilderment over the meaning of a juxtaposition on a neighbor's wall of a sword and a doll:

The child has nothing to which it can compare the situation. And everything that then was strange is even stranger in retrospect. The sum has been added up wrong and written down wrong and this faulty conclusion has long ago been accepted and approved. There's nothing to be done about it now.[10]

Because the story is concentrated in detail and imagery, it is difficult to summarize, but the persona remembers an incident when "Crazy Old Jack"—an eccentric old man who lived nearby and frightened the neighborhood children with his age and irritability and squalid way of living—came into her mother's kitchen. That her mother was not afraid but talked to him and gave him tea and food baffled her. Her mother was an enigma to her in other ways because of her habit of secrecy which caused the child to feel shut out. She describes her mother as being very much alone with a quick temper that often estranged the neighbors. When a neighbor did visit, the mother would ask her daughter to sit in the other room while she talked behind the closed door: "She closed the door as though she had said goodbye to me and to truth" (*DS*, 26). There is an image of the mother at the window in the mornings.

The window had sash curtains over its lower half. My mother's gaze was directed through the upper, uncurtained panes. Sometimes she would stand there for a long time, perfectly still, one hand on the window jamb, one hand hanging by her side. When she stood like this, she was puzzling to me; I knew nothing whatever about her; she was a stranger; I couldn't understand what she was. (*DS*, 25)

On one occasion when old Leonard came to visit, her mother opened the kitchen door and revealed to the daughter the old man sitting in the rocking chair peeling an apple. He smiled at her, but she was frightened by the bearded man ("I stood transfixed by that smile"). To add to her insecurity, he made a remark to her mother that mystified her:

"We must be wise," he said to my mother. "We must be as wise as the serpent and as gentle as the dove. As the serpent, as the dove," he said, and picked up the cup of tea from its saucer.

She says that she did not know the meaning of the words then and still does not.

It is such memories, compounded of bewilderment and ignorance and fear, that we must always keep in our hearts. We can never forget them because we cannot understand them, and because they are of no use. (*DS*, 26)[11]

The poem "Medusa," read with these concluding words in mind, evokes the feelings and imagery of the short story and of "Journey Around My Room." There is a mixture of protection and danger in the "house" in "a cave of trees" facing the "sheer" sky—an abyss. The "bell hung ready to strike" and the movement of light suggest the futility of time. In the house is the Medusa "Held up at the window, seen through a door." The image of the powerful, enigmatic mother at the window with her gaze "directed through the upper, uncurtained panes" comes to mind, in conjunction with the child's fear of the old man seen through a door ("I stood transfixed by that smile"). Even the serpents on the forehead hint at a possible emotional transference of Old Leonard's puzzling words: "We must be as wise as the serpent."

The Medusa poem compares as well with the dream ending "Journey Around My Room." In the dream, the persona confronts the danger of swimming the rapids and plunges into the wave that mounts "to the level of my eye." The universe swings up and is fallen into, as the sheer sky is faced and sun and reflection wheel by in "Medusa." She feels, in the dream, that she "must in a moment die" but first she sees all life containing hers raining over her and taking her down to "the translucent depths below fear" under the millstream—which she ties to the memory of the steam from the train that took her away from home to school at the age of eleven.

In the same manner, the persona of "Medusa" freezes in time after confronting the danger ("This is a dead scene forever now") among symbols of ongoing life, death, and seasons. The persona of "Medusa" stands "like a shadow" under "the great balanced day" as in the dream the persona is upheld and sees the "moment caught raining" over her. She sees "yellow dust" "lifting in the wind" that "does not drift away" as the dreamer saw the foam of the millstream and the child, the steam of the train.

Such personal emotion does not, by any means, narrow the meaning of the poem. Its symbolism, as in myth, universalizes the experience to deal with all terror of the overpowering and unknown. As Bogan said in a letter to Sister Angela:

> It is difficult to "explicate" one's own work—especially when the subject is lyric poetry. Let me say that lyric poetry is the most difficult gift there is: the most *exigent*. And it cannot be *faked*, like a good deal of other writing.
>
> . . . You will remember, I'm sure, in dealing with my work, that you are dealing with emotion under high pressure—so that *symbols* are its only release. [12]

Following "Medusa," with its concentrated, objectified emotion, is "Sub Contra," a call for the unleashing of repressed feeling—or the rage it causes. A stringed instrument under the control of the player is the metaphor for the emotions under the control of the mind, but it is also the expression of those emotions. In short, emphatic lines, the restrained sounds are compared to "the mockery in a shell," and the imperative statement is made, "Let there sound from music's root / One note rage can understand."

The Failure of Love

The remaining sixteen poems in the volume have to do with the difficulties of romantic love or passion, difficulties that appear insurmountable. A review of *Body of This Death* at the time of publication referred to "a tragedy that is not less impressive for being nameless" in her "love experience."[13] More than this, however, the concern of the poems is with the nature of romantic love and passion and its meaning to human existence rather than with a personal "tragedy." That alienation and loneliness are inherent in the man/woman relationship is the undercurrent of these poems. There is a poem, "Juan's Song," that was apparently written during this period but for some reason excluded from *Body of This Death* (only to be included with the *Body of This Death* poems in collected volumes) that should be considered here.[14] It is a poem about which Bogan later remarked in a letter to Sister Angela that "one can detect the bitterness which comes with a breakdown of early idealism":[15]

> When beauty breaks and falls asunder
> I feel no grief for it, but wonder.
> When love, like a frail shell, lies broken,
> I keep no chip of it for token.
> I never had a man for friend
> Who did not know that love must end.
> I never had a girl for lover
> Who could discern when love was over.
> What the wise doubt, the fool believes—
> Who is it, then, that love deceives?

"A Girl to Juan," evidently a companion poem, was published in the May 1924 *Measure*. Here the bitterness of the last lines—"and since she loves you, and she must, / Puts her young cheek against the dust"—is softened by the musical language and lyrical imagery of the poem as a whole.[16] The contrast with the bleakness of language of "Juan's Song" supports the meaning of that poem that men "know that love must end" while women cannot "discern when love [is] over." This theme—transitoriness, infidelity, disappointment—appears in many poems. Another theme is that of ensnarement, either of the man or of the woman, as in "The Frightened Man," "The Romantic," and "Sonnet." There are poems such as "Ad Castitatem," "The Crows," and "Stanza" that deal with the nature of passion itself, a "body of this death" in its disassociation with reciprocated love. Nowhere in these poems is there a happy love poem. Bogan's early poem "Betrothed" is reprinted here, but it suggests disappointment rather than hope. A hint of hope ends "The Changed Woman":

> And while she lives, the unwise, heady
> Dream, ever denied and driven,

> Will one day find her bosom ready,—
> That never thought to be forgiven.
>
> (22)

But as a whole the poem is rather bitter.

The nature of man and the nature of woman would appear to preclude real understanding and sympathy between the sexes, leaving all to the fate of loneliness or unhappiness. Bogan, at this young stage of her life, did not seem to question whether the experiences she invoked were inevitable. Her male personae shy away from real commitment, and her female personae try too hard to please and become resentful or expect too much. "Juan's Song," "The Frightened Man," and "The Romantic" offer a male view (as Bogan sees it) of women as adjunct or property in which female will is threatening. Women fare as badly. In "Women," Bogan outlines her objections to what she sees as the nature of their lives. The lines with parallel structure of the clauses, repetition of "they," and the stanza-ending, short, bitter descriptions read like an indictment. The imagery is of restriction and experiential bankruptcy for women: women "have no wilderness in them." The imagery is of the open world—nature, journeys, profit, self-esteem—for men. Women's "love is an eager meaninglessness / Too tense, or too lax" and the remedy perhaps is in imitating the detachment Bogan attributes to men.

"Memory" juxtaposes this attitude to the romantic view of memory (presumedly that of a love affair) as gloriously or tragically undying. The poem begins with "Do not guard this as rich stuff without mark" and ends with the stanza:

> Rather, like shards and straw upon coarse ground,
> Of little worth when found,—
> Rubble in gardens, it and stones alike,
> That any spade may strike.
>
> (18)

The underlying bitterness of these words is also evident in "Men Loved Wholly Beyond Wisdom" in which women's love is "like a fire in a dry thicket" that men must return, and the wise course is not to love in this reckless way but

> To be quiet in the fern
> Like a thing gone dead and still,

> Listening to the prisoned cricket
> Shake its terrible, dissembling
> Music in the granite hill.
>
> (16)

The detachment advised has a price. But, even so, detachment as goal
is explored in two poems that Bogan later dropped from the collections. One is quite long and rather rambling. Written in free verse,
it is titled "A Letter" and is directed to a rejecting lover from the
countryside where she has come to recuperate.[17] The poem has some
lovely lines, such as these beginning the second stanza:

> This is a countryside of roofless houses,—
> Taverns to rain,—doorsteps of millstones, lintels
> Leaning and delicate, foundations sprung to lilacs,
> Orchards where boughs like roots strike into the sky.
> Here I could well devise the journey to nothing

But the thought is loose and unfocused and the mood uncertain. The
last stanza begins with words that echo Eliot: "Shall I play the pa-
vanne / For a dead child or the scene where that girl / Lets fall her
hair. . . ." and ends "abstinence, beauty is nothing, / That you re-
gret me, that I feign defiance / And now I have written you this, it
is nothing."

Bogan later explained her dissatisfaction with the poem to John
Hall Wheelock who was editing a collection of her poems, *Poems and
New Poems:*

—I don't think, however, that we can keep "A Letter." There is something
wrong with it; I can't say just what. Something sentimental or unfinished
or mawkish. Whatever it is, I don't like it. So please let's take it out.—I
don't like "Love me because I am lost," either. Don't you think we might
dispense with that, as well?

It isn't that I'm turning on my early self. But the girl of 23 and 24, who
wrote most of these early poems, was so seldom mawkish, that I want her
not to be mawkish at all.—[18]

In the discussion of "Love me because I am lost" ("Song") in connection with Bogan's use of form, I suggested that Bogan was unaware
of why she thought the poem mawkish. In the case of "A Letter," I
believe she is closer to accuracy in her assessment, but she still misses

the emotional and mental confusion that makes the poem "unfinished." There is sentimentality, too, but disequilibrium operates
more often.

The other poem to be dropped is in the same vein. Entitled
"Words for Departure,"[19] it is also mixed in feeling. Recommending
a coolly deliberate parting ("And go away without fire or lantern. /
Let there be some uncertainty about your departure"), it still has a
note of longing for permanence. The middle section, or strophe, of
the three-part, free-verse poem is in contrast in emotional tone to the
first and last sections. It begins: "I have remembered you. / You were
not the town visited once, / Nor the road falling behind running
feet."

These are the poems of a poet flailing around for a point of view or
focus of feeling rather than creating either. Bogan was right in rejecting them as not representative of her work. Much better is a short
poem near the end of *Body of This Death* that admits the self-decep-
tion of her pose of indifference. Like "Song" it is in the form of a
musical lyric, but the irony of the form is recognized:

Chanson un peu naïve

What body can be ploughed,
Sown, and broken yearly?
She would not die, she vowed,
But she has, nearly.
   Sing, heart, sing;
   Call and carol clearly.

And, since she could not die,
Care would be a feather,
A film over the eye
Of two that lie together.
   Fly, song, fly,
   Break your little tether.

So from strength concealed
She makes her pretty boast:
Pain is a furrow healed
And she may love you most.
   Cry, song, cry,
   And hear your crying lost.
         (23)

The seriousness of the desolation makes this poem uncomfortable in its bitter form, however; and it remains for the last two poems in the book, "Fifteenth Farewell" and "Sonnet," to address the problem with the integration of form, imagery, and sound that most successfully makes the poet's feeling available to others.

The Poem as Last Resort

"Sonnet" ("Since you would claim the sources of my thought") is placed in italics on the last page. The italics indicate a summation or point of arrival—an emphasis of some kind, as does its position as the final poem. The order in which poems appear in the book has significance if we are to assume that Bogan included her own works in a statement made in an article, "Reading Contemporary Poetry": "Any collected or selected volume will present poems in the order in which the poet has decided they should be read; and this is the order to follow."[20]

Reading the poems in order, we find that the poet has begun with "A Tale" and the fear implicit in aspiration followed by "Medusa" with its feeling of paralyzing, defeating forces followed immediately by a call to liberating rage ("Sub Contra"). Next come the poems that examine the failure of romantic love, going from the confused feeling of personal rejection in "A Letter" and "Words for Departure"—separated from one another by "The Frightened Man" and "Betrothed," both expressing disappointment—to an attempt at philosophical rejection of passion ("Ad Castitatem" and "Knowledge") to those poems seeing the pain of loss in relation to the nothingness of death ("Portrait," "My Voice Not Being Proud," "Statue and Birds," "Epitaph for a Romantic Woman"). The difficulties of intellectually freeing oneself from feeling are explored in "The Alchemist," "Men Loved Wholly Beyond Wisdom," and "The Crows." A bitter rebellion against one-sided emotional attachment in "Memory" and "Women" is followed by the recognition that individuality has a price in "Last Hill in a Vista." "Song," "Stanza," "The Changed Woman," and "Chanson un peu naïve" in quite different ways deal with disillusionment and discouragement in finding happiness in a romantic relationship.

"Fifteenth Farewell," with its recognition of the nature of loneliness as being more than the lack of another presence, is placed before "Sonnet," the concluding italicized poem which proclaims the necessity of freedom of thought at whatever price.

So we have come full circle back to the urgency and danger of aspiration in the face of societal demands, first those of the parents and then those of a mate. Despite the pain and denial necessitated, there is really no alternative to escape from these demands—from "the body of this death"—if the poet is to maintain her emotional and intellectual integrity. Yet, the conclusion is a desperate one that implies an underlying desire to comprehend and a hope of finding a more satisfactory means of living, of attaining both personal development and human understanding.

In 1923, when *Body of This Death* was published, Bogan was twenty-six years old and struggling to overcome the emotional difficulties of childhood trauma and insecurity compounded by the disappointments of her marriage and ensuing relationships with men. Her later journals make it plain that the emotionally and economically unstable, and socially isolated, nature of her parents' marriage had a violent, lasting effect upon her.[21] Although her feelings toward her mother, as a result, were deeply ambivalent, her daughter, Maidie Alexander Scannell, told me in November 1974 that Bogan's mother was very proud of her. Because Scannell's father, Curt Alexander, died in 1920 and Bogan had separated from him before that, Scannell was unable to offer light on that relationship. But Bogan, herself, in a letter to Morton Zabel in 1937, had this to say of her youth:

I never was a member of a "lost generation." I was the highly charged and neurotically inclined product of an extraordinary childhood and an unfortunate early marriage, into which state I had rushed to escape the first. . . . I had no relations whatever with the world about me; I lived in a dream, populated by figures out of Maeterlinck and Pater and Arthur Symons and Compton Mackenzie (*Sinister Street* and *Sylvia Scarlett* made a great impression on me) and H. G. Wells and Francis Thompson and Alice Meynell and Swinburne and John Masefield and other oddly assorted authors. What I did and what I felt was, I assure you, *sui generis*.[22]

One who has no relationship to the world about her feels herself different from the approved societal model and beyond the understanding of others, but no less in need of understanding. In this situation, an emotional paralysis, a neurosis, can truly become a "body of this death" as "Medusa" portrays.

In December of the same year as the publication of *Body of This Death,* Bogan wrote a few thoughts on the nature of poetic creation

for the *New Republic*. They begin, "When he sets out to resolve, as
rationally as he may, the tight irrational knot of his emotion, the
poet hesitates for a moment"; she then proceeds to describe the nature
of the poetic impulse. "The poem is always a last resort," Bogan says.
A true effort requires facing feeling and dealing only with essentials,
not flinching away to synthetic writing, "even though at its best a
poem cannot come straight out of the heart, but must break away in
some oblique fashion from the body of sorrow or joy,—be the mask,
not the incredible face." Under such restraint, passion must "achieve
its own form, definite and singular."[23] The pursuit of perfection, of
the ideal, is a lonely, discouraging business, especially for a young
woman reared in a male society.

Chapter Five
Dark Summer

A Changing Perspective

The period between the publication of *Body of This Death* in 1923 and her next book, *Dark Summer,* in 1929 was for Bogan a time of both poetic growth and impending emotional problems. While her letters show her to be very much occupied with literature and writing, there seems to have been a reluctance as well—a fear of the intensity of creativity. She wrote toward the end of a letter to Rolfe Humphries in July 1924, "O God, why were women born with ambition! I wish I could sit and tat, instead of wanting to go and write THE poem, or lie and kiss the ground."[1] And in another letter to him in August, "To hell with art! It's a waste of time, and besides, it breaks my heart. Go away, little girl, I won't buy your damned violets."[2] Both remarks were made in a context that might qualify their being taken seriously, but she made no bones about being emotionally upset at times during this period.

She married Raymond Holden, the poet and novelist, in July 1925, and suggests in her letters that she was both happy and anxious in the relationship, anxious because homemaking was another pull away from writing. On the one hand, she was saying in a letter to Ruth Benedict, the anthropologist, in August:

We have taken a little apartment with a big sunny *kitchen*—you see, I did get one after all. It's going to be extremely jolly, and I must admit that domesticity thrills me to the bone. Yesterday I made peach jam![3]

On the other hand, she writes in a letter to Benedict the following April: "Margaret [Mead] I have neglected most shamefully. My letters would have been so domestic, and she would have so girned and girded at me."[4] She signs the letter, "Ever, the domestic and vanishing Bogan." In the same letter, she mentions that she has been invited to Yaddo, an artists' colony in Saratoga Springs, New York, and might go for the month of August. "Would I work?" she asks.

She did go and she did work. One of the poems written there was "Dark Summer," the title poem of her second volume.[5] I believe that a close look at the poem provides insight into the volume as a whole. That the seasonal summer is a metaphor for the summer of life is indicated by the human terms in which the images of nature are presented. The storm is "not yet heard," the lightning "not yet found," the apples are "for the late comer." The last lines are completely in human terms of "spell," "rite," and "kisses." The summer of life brings confrontation with the ineffable quality of existence as both beckoning and bound up in a force beyond human control, a force that threatens the fruits of life. I believe that Bogan felt threatened as an individual in addition to sharing the human lot.

The next to the last line—"The simple spell, the rite not for our word"—is suggestive of Emily Dickinson and like Dickinson has religious overtones. But Bogan's Irish-Catholic religious background and her feelings about thunder were more like those of Joyce than those of Dickinson. She wrote Rolfe Humphries in 1924, "The lightning startles me merely, the thunder would wring me with fright were I a mole underground."[6] The fear perhaps is one of retribution, of God's punishment, and in this poem it casts a spell over the fruits of maturity. Are the "kisses not for our mouths" love withheld from the undeserving? Whatever the nature of the fear, it is fear that darkens the summer.

The poems gathered together under the title of *Dark Summer* view the world from the point of early maturity, a time of changing perspective. In an unpublished short story, "Half a Letter," Bogan would later describe youth as the time of living in the future, seen in dramatic, important terms. But when older, "we are literally ourselves, and things function literally around us, terribly apparent and undisguised."[7] Her poems written at this time are less concerned with romantic love and more deeply metaphysical in nature than the earlier poems. Some of them reflect the neurotic fears that were building. Two lines from a later poem, "After the Persian," may describe how she felt about these years: "I have wept with the spring storm; / Burned with the brutal summer."

Intellectual Analysis of Feeling

The volume consists of twenty-three new short poems and two long poems. (There are also ten reprinted poems from *Body of This Death* inserted in the middle of the book because John Hall Wheelock, the editor, apparently thought the book should be longer.)[8] Comprising the poems in section 2 of *The Blue Estuaries* with the addition of the long poem "The Flume," they are arranged into section 1, "Winter Swan" through "Simple Autumnal"; section 2, "The Flume"; section 3, the poems from *Body of This Death;* section 4, "Dark Summer" through "Old Countryside" (with the order reversed for "Didactic Piece" and "For a Marriage" and also for "The Crossed Apple" and "Song for a Slight Voice"); and section 5, "Summer Wish." Bogan once defined metaphysical poems as "meditations on time, being, essence," a definition that fits most of the poems in this volume.[9]

However, when noting the influence on Bogan of poets of earlier centuries, critics usually see the lyrical attributes rather than the metaphysical as the inheritance in her poetry. Yvor Winters in his review of *Dark Summer* for the *New Republic* saw her as "progressing toward a more purely lyrical mode that culminates in 'The Mark,' 'Come break with time,' and 'Simple Autumnal'; poems that demand—and will bear—comparison with the best songs of the sixteenth and seventeenth centuries, whether one selects examples from Campion, Jonson, or Dryden."[10] Theodore Roethke echoed this assessment when he said, "But for the most part she writes out of the severest lyrical tradition in English. Her real spiritual ancestors are Campion, Jonson, the anonymous Elizabethan song writers."[11] And Ford Madox Ford, while recognizing the more analytical metaphysicals, emphasized the public Herrick and Marvell as comparison when reviewing *The Sleeping Fury* in 1937:

There is, in fact, everything that goes to the making of one of those more pensive seventeenth century, usually ecclesiastical English poets who are the real glory of our twofold lyre. Miss Bogan may—and probably will—stand somewhat in a quiet landscape that contains George Herbert, and Donne and Vaughan, and why not even Herrick? This is not to be taken as appraisement. It is neither the time nor the place to say that Miss Bogan ranks with Marvell.[12]

It is true that Bogan uses many of the forms of these early poets, but her poems are essentially different. She is not a social poet but an introspective poet—however objectively she may present the results of her introspection. She is also a poet of ideas, as has been recognized; yet Winters further says in his review, "The intricacy of some of the best of Miss Bogan's poems is, I imagine, an intricacy of feeling, and hence of style rather than of idea" (*NR*, 247), and Roethke refers to "complexity and depth" (*MQR*, 249) in a context of emotional impact that slights the intellectual element of the impact. It is the intellectual analysis of feeling that makes for intricacy in many of Bogan's poems.

"Winter Swan," for example, the first poem in *Dark Summer*, sees in the swan in winter the idea of mutability, but the idea is prompted by emotion: "Within the mind the live blood shouts aloud." It is the despair of passing time that causes the persona to see the garden scene as "hollow," a despair expressed directly in the lines "Where lies the leaf-caught world once thought abiding, / Now but a dry disarray and artifice?" But the despair seeks an answer, or reason, and it is the synthesis of emotion and thought that perceives the swan as containing the enigma in the rich imagery of the last two lines. The image of the swan very probably occurred to Bogan as a result of having previously read Yeats's "The Wild Swans at Coole," but it is a measure of her intellectualization that she probes more deeply the implications of the symbol with the result that the emotional impact is also deeper.[13] The verb *drift* ("But now they drift on the still water, / Mysterious, beautiful"),[14] used by Yeats in the last stanza of his poem, becomes more forceful with "the ripple cut by the cold" (the drift to death) in Bogan's poem. A comparison with Yeats's poem illustrates, in addition, Bogan's objective concentration of words that is more similar to Donne's manner than to the personal narrative of Yeats's poem.

Mutability

Bogan analyzed in other poems and by other symbols the feelings engendered by mutability. In "Division" (32), the passage of time brings destruction to the "single," but the "whole" remains. The hour, season, and the mutability they bring are symbolized by the long shadow cast by the tree:

> The tree and the hour and the shadow
> No longer mingle,
> Fly free, that burned together.

The shadow and the leaves it reflects disappear with a little time, but time itself and the tree remain. That this mutability is a matter of human concern is apparent in the emotion of the phrase "that burned together," giving intensity to the moment when the "tree and the hour and the shadow" mingled, and in the emotion of the adjectives "assailed and undone," deploring the disappearance of the leaves and their shadow. The "burden of the seen / Is clasped against the eye" of the poet—not a casual expression of observation—in the interpretation of the division of the tree into its shadow by time as the division of universal life into individual life by time.

By contrast, the lack of emotion in "The Cupola" (34) recreates the indifference of nature to the destruction of the single, the particular. Death is brought into the human abode, "the shuttered room," in a "handsbreath of darkest reflection" as a mirror on the wall catches the image of boughs and drifted leaves. "Someone" has hung the mirror "for no reason" but

> Someone has thought alike of the bough and the wind
> And struck their shape to the wall. Each in its season
> Spills negligent death throughout the abandoned chamber.

Bogan effectively uses free-verse lines in this poem to create an impression of dispassion by the lack of the emotional stimuli of a regular beat and of rhyme.

Nature may be indifferent, but the individual cannot be and survive; and it is the tragedy of human life that the mind is aware of the natural process to death while the emotions are involved in sheer living, in the will to prevail. "Simple Autumnal" is concerned with this tragedy and the grief it engenders. Here, the sonnet form allows the expression of feeling in beat and rhyme along with the working of idea in the metaphors of cyclic nature and the personifications of grief and sorrow, culminating in a final couplet: "Full season's come, yet filled trees keep the sky / And never scent the ground where they must lie."

Despite feelings of indomitability, the drive for life is defeated eventually. That man is a mark of fate, of "time's long treason," is the bleak theme of "The Mark." It begins:

> Where should he seek, to go away
> That shadow will not point him down?
> The spear of dark in the strong day
> Beyond the upright body thrown,
> Marking no epoch but its own.
>
> (38)

This is one of the poems that Winters compared as song to Campion, Jonson, or Dryden. It is true that music is a component, although the rhythm, especially in the third stanza, is roughened by thought. Bogan herself referred to the poem as "contemplative," and to me the thought takes it out of the class of the purely lyrical.[15]

Another poem on a similar theme she saw also in terms of thought, "Didactic Piece" (42). She wrote Rolfe Humphries on December 27, 1925: "A new poem is rapidly coming on, to be called 'Didactic Piece,' but really nothing but the title can be divulged at this moment because I don't know anything else about it myself."[16] A typescript of the completed poem is stamped with the date April 7, 1927, by the recipient *Poetry* magazine and carries in Bogan's handwriting the Santa Fe, New Mexico, address where she was living at that time. "For R." is also indicated in Bogan's handwriting, presumably a dedication to her husband, Raymond. In a letter of May 23, 1927, to Harriet Monroe, editor of *Poetry*, Bogan wrote, "It was nice of you to take the poem. It is obscure, but that's the way it came."[17]

As is not surprising, given a didactic intent, the free verse in places sounds prosy, but the underlying poignancy of the lesson—the necessity to recognize that life is limited by death—serves to create an overall lyricism of expression, both in rhythm and metaphor. In the last stanza a harp represents the emotions or spirit that must be heeded yet controlled, and death itself is "the eyeless music."

The weight of death on life becomes such that it is seen as affording "cruel ease" in "Come, Break with Time," a poem that has fast, short lines suggesting a ticking or chiming clock. The last stanza, with lines that are a little slower and longer, reminds one of the second stanza of Wordsworth's "A Slumber Did My Spirit Seal":

> No motion has she now, no force;
> She neither hears nor sees;
> Rolled round in earth's diurnal course,
> With rocks, and stones, and trees.

Roethke, marking the resemblance, commented: "Notice the remarkable shift in rhythm in the last stanza, with the run-on lines that pick up the momentum of the poem. We are caught up in the earth's whole movement; I am reminded, perhaps eccentrically, of Wordsworth's [stanza above]. In this instance, I feel one poem supports, gives additional credence, to the other" (*MQR*, 248).

But unlike the dead Lucy of Wordsworth's poem, Bogan's subject is "rolled round in earth's diurnal course" while still alive. It is "earth's heavy measure" that makes the life span insignificant and the "clock's chime" ironic. Bogan's poem does not mourn for the loss of an individual, but for the fate of the human single in a vast and indifferent design. It is not the loss of life so much as the loss of a quality of life that the poem treats. Time lords, burns like a brand, and decrees.

"Sonnet" ("Dark, underground, is furnished with the bone"), another poem on the subject of death, also treats the quality of life rather than the end of life in that its theme is the temporality of endeavor and experience except for the scars that remain. The weight of meaning seems to be that pain is the principal characteristic of life, so prevailing that it is not destroyed by death. Since the scars are scars of the psyche rather than of the body and therefore as mortal as endeavor or experience, they function as a metaphor for the nature of life as it appears to the poet (48).

Religion

Aspiration is nullified by inexorable time and the mutability it brings, and death, the "eyeless music," holds no comfort for the single. That Bogan rejects the traditional Christian concept of a life after death is apparent in "I Saw Eternity," a bitter but funny response to the seventeenth-century poet Henry Vaughn whose "The World," *Silex Scintillan,* begins:

> I saw Eternity the other night,
> Like a great *Ring* of pure and endless light,
>   All calm, as it was bright,
> And round beneath it, Time in hours, days, years
>   Driv'n by the spheres
> Like a vast shadow mov'd, In which the world
>   And all her train were hurl'd.

Bogan's lines are a repudiation of a concept which she denounces as having "spoiled my mind":

> O beautiful Forever!
> O grandiose Everlasting!
> Now, now, now,

I break you into pieces,
I feed you to the ground.

O brilliant, O languishing
Cycle of weeping light!
The mice and birds will eat you,
And you will spoil their stomachs
As you have spoiled my mind.

Here, mice, rats,
Porcupines and toads,
Moles, shrews, squirrels,
Weasels, turtles, lizards,—
Here's bright Everlasting!
Here's a crumb of Forever!
Here's a crumb of Forever!

(50)

Far from Vaughn's view of Christianity as offering consolation during life and haven after death, Bogan views the religion she was reared in as causing trouble during life and offering nothing afterward. The view is not held without pain, although Bogan could trivialize her major concerns with flippancy as in an unsigned poem published in 1926 in the New Yorker called "Consolations of Religion," with the subtitle "By a Reincarnationist," in which she entertains the possibility of being a pollywog.[18] Her rebellion was more complex than flippancy or bitterness, nevertheless, as is made evident in a later poem ("Old Divinity") in the New Yorker, this time signed with her initials, which has as its first stanza:

If you at length remain
Though all your garlands wilt—
Awake in me, like pain,
Afire in me, like guilt—[19]

Bogan's definition of metaphysical poetry as that which deals with "time, being, essence" does not mention religion as such; her metaphysical poetic concerns are with understanding or comprehending the nature of existence as modified by time rather than with embracing or arguing an established dogma. Emotion rather than thought leads her to seek comprehension, of course—the pain and guilt that will not accede to her rational judgment. It is the problem of the psyche aspiring to that which the mind finds impossible, whether it be life, love, or early faith.

The Self

Bogan looks for essence behind and beyond traditional ways of seeing the world and behind her own experience, often dealing with the subconscious as a key to essence. Her poems in *Dark Summer* explore the struggle to understand self as well as to understand the universe. Some deal with romantic love or passion, but except for "Girl's Song," a reprint of the 1924 "A Girl to Juan," the emphasis is on self-understanding in love. "For a Marriage" is especially self-concerned but is written in the third person to describe a psychological state (43). The state described, one of fearful reticence in a close relationship, was to be a factor in Bogan's later emotional illness. Related to her problem with jealousy and childhood anxieties, it was to be struggled with at length before being overcome. The poem suffers, in my understanding of it, from the metaphor of the sword as the sight allowed of her nature. I find it confusing, if expressive of the danger she feels in being revealed. The poem itself is as obscure and knotted in symbol as her feelings were.

"Song for a Slight Voice" is similar, if less tense, in its description of her troubled feelings of inadequacy and fear. As she does often, she has used the form of a song, this time with music as metaphor for the harmony of understanding, and the rhythm of the first and last stanzas moves easily. The middle stanza with the anguish most openly expressed moves less easily. That she described her voice as "slight" in the title hints at her fears of failure to relate, as does the noun *plunder:*

> If ever I render back your heart
> So long to me delight and plunder,
> It will be bound with the firm strings
> That men have built the viol under.
>
> Your stubborn, piteous heart, that bent
> To be the place where music stood,
> Upon some shaken instrument
> Stained with the dark of resinous blood,

> Will find its place, beyond denial,
> Will hear the dance, O be most sure,
> Laid on the curved wood of the viol
> Or on the struck tambour.
>
> (47)

The meaning lies within the metaphor, as her true feelings lie within her subconscious. Bogan had faith in the subconscious as a guide to understanding, but used it with caution. As she was to say in a later review, "The subconscious, when dredged up without skill or imagination, can be every bit as tiresome as the conscious."[20] Without looking for the inherent meaning, she did not look at all.

Sleep and dream as elements of the subconscious, or unconscious, can provide symbols and metaphors for Bogan's poems, as in "Second Song," a poem about passion. The rhythm and rhyme are incantatory as though casting a spell. "Passion" is addressed on the level of magic, the irrational level where it exists. In "Feuer-Nacht," which Roethke thought remarkable for the powerful way in which the theme builds, passion is not directly addressed, but the fire is known to be metaphor by the use of the word *sworn* in the beginning. The short, fast-moving lines support the imagery of the sweeping fire:

> The leaf-veined fire,
> Sworn to trouble the least
> The shuttered eye
> Turned from its feast,—
>
> (36)

In still another poem, "The Drum," another metaphor and another rhythm present a more direct statement, ending in the last stanza with the first person, "It's the drums I'll have." In both "Feuer-Nacht" and "The Drum" the metaphor determines the imagery, line, and rhythm to create quite different treatments of a similar theme.

"The Crossed Apple" is an even more different treatment. Bogan explains on a recorded reading that this poem is based on the fairy story of a witch who brings a young girl an apple, one side of which is poisoned.[21] Again, the extended metaphor controls all elements of the poem. The rhythm and phrasing suggest that used by witches in fairy stories, and life as a "crossed apple" has both the ordinary, nourishing qualities of apples and the magical, threatening qualities that the witch suggests. The young girl is offered the red side, Sweet

Burning; the witch keeps the white side, Meadow Milk. This feeling of a supernatural separation of "the fire and the breast" to the exclusion of the desirable is also in "Dark Summer," as are apples in another context: "The apples that hang and swell for the late comer, / The simple spell, the rite not for our word, / The kisses not for our mouths,—light the dark summer."

"The Flume"

The emotional insecurities and fears that underlie "Dark Summer" and "The Crossed Apple" are made more evident in a long poem called "The Flume."[22] In four parts, it covers eleven pages of the small volume. It is not a good poem, to my mind, although there are good lines, because—as Bogan herself later said—"The 'facts' are false, at the end." The "facts" are wrong because the poem represents an attempt to solve rationally an irrational state that is not understood. Unlike "Medusa," which deals only on the level of the subconscious with an authentic emotional experience, "The Flume" constructs a fictional frame around the subconscious experiences that imposes a synthetic meaning upon them. Imagery that appears in other poems and stories, seemingly derived from Bogan's childhood, appears here again bound up with the themes of jealousy, guilt, and fear. There is the flume, the noisy spill of water over the mill's dam, the mirror reflecting scenes from outdoors into her room; and a long description, all of part 2, of her terrible fear of thunder. Apparently it was the fear that inspired the poem. She said in a letter of July 22, 1924, to Rolfe Humphries, "I want to do a lyric called 'Thunder.' Did you ever have that kind of mindless, idealess compulsion—that you must do a lyric called 'Thunder' (or any other name)?"[23] Two days later she wrote, "Today I hope to finish my lightning passage. I'll send it to you—since you're a brother in fright."[24]

The protagonist of the poem, a young married woman, is described in lines like the opening line in part 1, "She had a madness in her for betrayal," and the closing lines, "She had some guilt in her to be betrayed, / She had the terrible hope he could not love her." Her face seen in a mirror is "The young face, softly marred by its own derision." In another letter to Humphries on August 28, Bogan belittled the poem:

Will you listen to the first cantos of my narrative—which probably will go down the ages in the *Christabel* class? I am going to finish the lightning part, and call it a day, I think. I've lost all interest in the woman in it, who used to rush around the house hoping she'd be betrayed. I'm sure she's been betrayed by this time and has taken to washing dishes and having babies, like any other milky-breasted female, married to a he-man.[25]

But she worked at it and on September 6 wrote, "The lightning's done, as I have before intimated. There's only going to be one more part, making four in all."[26] It was published as "The Flume" in the *Measure* the following June (1925). It was not included in any of the volumes of poetry after *Dark Summer,* however, because Bogan had come to feel that it was "false."

The Subconscious

When Bogan writes directly from her subconscious or unconscious experiences, on the other hand, as she did with "Medusa," her poems have a power that transcends the individual pysche. "Late," "Tears in Sleep," "Fiend's Weather," and "Old Countryside" are such poems. Vivid imagery and compression of expression invoke the mysterious battles of the mind, either in sleep, as in "Late" and "Tears in Sleep," or in neuroses or haunting childhood impressions, as in "Fiend's Weather" and "Old Countryside."

"Late" is a stark picture of primal fears in which the world is seen as menacing, and the protagonist has the irrational perception of dream ("Now sullen and deranged"). There is nightmare imagery of a screaming cormorant over a cave and a rocky promontory, of "stony wings." Basic fears of destruction of the self are here; but here is also the awareness of the disappointed adult ("Not simply, as a child") who finds glory to be "bleak" and embattled and who can mock the cold sterility of the earth. The coldness is the destruction of the mature self who in dream is menaced by the loss of childhood wonder and faith without the concomitant loss of childhood fears. Indeed, the fear felt is the same throughout.

"Tears in Sleep," while bearing on a personal anxiety, the painful problem of the inability to accept love that is besieging Bogan during this period, is haunting in its evocation of the hold of a dream against awakening. The imagery of "the cage of sleep" and "I clung to the bars of the dream" is so right, as is the impact of the poem as a whole, because beyond its individual cause, it contacts the nature of dream (44).

"Fiend's Weather" is a visualization of a conflicting emotional state—in this case an unhealthy fear that happiness brings—accurately described as "weather" because it is the climate of the spirit, not a conscious process of the mind, and will both storm and abate:

> O embittered Joy,
> You fiend in fair weather,
> Foul winds from secret quarters
> Howl here together.
>
> They yell without sleet
> And freeze without snow;
> Through them the broken Pleiades
> And the Brothers show,
>
> And Orion's steel,
> And the iron of the Plough.
> This is your night, my worthy fiend,
> You can triumph now.
>
> In this wind to wrench the eye
> And curdle the ear,
> The church steeple rises purely to the heavens;
> The sky is clear.
>
> And even to-morrow
> Stones without disguise
> In true-colored fields
> Will glitter for your eyes.
>
> (49)

The last poem in part 4, and the last short poem in the volume (part 5 is the long poem "Summer Wish"), is "Old Countryside" (52). Imagery of Bogan's childhood impressions that reappear in her writing are compacted into a quietly building mood of dread.[27] The question of the first poem in the volume, "Winter Swan"—"Where lies the leaf-caught world once thought abiding, / Now but a dry disarray and artifice?"—is asked again by implication. The summer thunder, the cloudy day, the bell, the mirrors reflecting the outdoors indoors, the shell, the scrawled vine, the red thorns of the rose branch—all these images are in other poems and are central to Bogan's meaning. The enigmatic "all has come to proof" of the second line is followed by "The summer thunder, like a wooden bell, / Rang in the storm . . .": the fears of childhood seem to have materialized in maturity, making the summer of life dark and the inevitable winter fearful. However, without relating to, or even recognizing, Bogan's private meaning, the reader finds that the poem evokes a poignant recognition of the precariousness of existence.

"Summer Wish"

In the long poem "Summer Wish" (53–59) concluding the volume, Bogan tries to come to terms with this precariousness and her own anxieties. The title and the form of a dialogue are inspired by Yeats's lament for Robert Gregory, "Shepherd and Goatherd," from which is taken the epigraph: "That cry's from the first cuckoo of the year. / I wished before it ceased." Bogan, in recording her reading of the poem, explained that one voice is that of nature and the other that of human experience. In his discussion on the record jacket, Harold Bloom has this to say: "Two voices speak in alternation . . . with the passionate soul expressing its longings, and the observant self describing the phenomena of its mutable world moving slowly towards summer, the season desired by the soul. The two voices fail consistently to heed the other, in an extended ironic vision of the divided psyche."[28]

I disagree that the two voices fail to heed the other or that the poem represents "an extended ironic vision of the divided psyche." Quite the contrary, I find that the second voice (nature) reflects the first (human experience) in a working through by the poet of old fears and loss of hope to a point where they can be seen as a part of the universal cycle with the same promise of renewal. Throughout, the psychic state or observation of the first voice is put into the perspective of the cyclic pattern of nature by the second voice.

Beginning with the words "We call up the green to hide us / This hardened month," the first voice asks for hope from the coming season, although experience has diminished expectation. The response of the second voice (nature) is to describe the March season in terms of cold presaging summer, and ends:

> Later, the sprung moss
> Is the tree's shadow; under the black spruces
> It lies where lately snow lay, bred green from the cold
> Cast down from melting branches.

The revitalization of nature is parallel to the yearning of the human psyche despite its weariness: "The wish from summer as always: *It will be, / It will be.*"

The first voice says that it can no longer believe in hope: "A wish like a hundred others. / You cannot, as once, yearn forward." And the second voice tells her to "Count over what these days have: lilies / Returned in little to an earth unready, / To the sun not accountable." The first voice begins the long look into the old fears and bitternesses that blight the prospect of life: "Memory long since put by,—to what end the dream / That drags back lived-out life with the wrong words, / The substitute meaning?" Old, unhappy relationships prey on the present—her dead husband who cannot explain and, above all, her painful childhood experience with her mother. (May Sarton refers to that pain when she describes Bogan as "an Irish Catholic child living with an overpowering mother's rages.")[29] The present cannot be free of the past because she has not finished with it; she has borne "the blow too young." Nature, the second voice, points out the unsteady April sunlight, "Light there's no use for," that is too early to prevail:

> In early April
> At six o'clock the sun has not set; on the walls
> It shines with scant light, pale, dilute, misplaced,
> Light there's no use for. At overcast noon
> The sun comes out in a flash, and is taken
> Slowly back to the cloud.

The first voice despairs of love when unreasoning jealousy interferes; and the second voice describes a shadow that darkens and lifts:

> The cloud shadow flies up the bank, but does not
> Blow off like smoke. It stops at the bank's edge.
> In the field by trees two shadows come together.
> The trees and the cloud throw down their shadow upon
> The man who walks there. Dark flows up from his feet
> To his shoulders and throat, then has his face in its mask,
> Then lifts.

The first voice sees no hope in overcoming the wounds that dominate the personality. In lines remarkable for their insight into the nature of neurosis, the conflict is described in its power to rule by means of a Medusa-like image, "a vision too strong / Ever to turn away." The second voice replies in a manner to indicate that nature absorbs the residue of a season and goes on to the next. Children play in the lengthening day ("The evening takes their cry"), and blossoms grow "around old weeds worn thin."

The first voice, enlarging upon her tendency to "Clot up the bone of phrase with the black conflict / That claws it back from sense," recognizes that the subconscious is not always apparent to the reason nor subject to the will:

> The mind for refuge, the grain of reason, the will,
> Pulled by a wind it thinks to point and name?
> Malicious symbol, key for rusty wards,
> The crafty knight in the game, with its mixed move,
> Prey to an end not evident to craft. . . .

The second voice in portraying the process of plowing a field ("inward from edge to center"), suggests that the thinking process works in a like manner (". . . to the center where the team turns last. / Horses in half-ploughed fields / Make earth they walk upon a changing color"). Encouraged at last, the first voice decides to hope again rather than to nurse "the bane that cheats the heart." In nature's renewal there is hope of parallel psychic renewal ("Speak it [the wish], as that man said, *as though the earth spoke*"). And the poem ends with the second voice: "See now / Open above the field, stilled in wing-stiffened flight, / The stretched hawk fly."

Harold Bloom remarks that "the second voice completes the poem with the Yeatsian figure of the hawk's flight as an image both of acceptance and of the effort to hold oneself open to experience." In this, I agree. But, although there is acceptance, hope is still qualified ("Though it be but for sleep at night, / Speak out the wish"). Many years later, Bogan was to explain her view of nature in relation to human life:

Are not trees and skies and water and earth, nature; to which man is added: *Homo additus naturae?* To which human life is added, and from which it is not wholly (certainly) derived. And with human life we get all the significant blood and the tears. And the gift of the intellect. And the common law. And art. The same current runs through the whole set-up—natural and human: true. But in man the power is transformed; and it is this transformation with which we must deal. The trees and the stones and the sea serve us as symbols, and stand around us like brothers and sisters—but they are inhuman siblings. . . .[30]

Nature serves as symbols to human life; nevertheless, the human must determine what the symbols mean.

Bloom calls "Summer Wish" Bogan's "Resolution and Independence." Because both poems concern poets at maturity, fearful of the future, they make for an interesting comparison between nineteenth- and twentieth-century life views. In Wordsworth's poem, the poet is happily walking on the moor one beautiful morning—"The pleasant season did my heart employ: / My old remembrances went from me wholly; / And all the ways of men, so vain and melancholy"—when his happiness suddenly precipitates a depression: "And fears and fancies thick upon me came; / Dim sadness—and blind thoughts, I knew not, nor could name." He fears that his past happiness and lack of care may end in a future day of "Solitude, pain of heart, distress, and poverty." The nature of the poet isn't to be practical: "By our own spirits are we deified; / We Poets in our youth begin in gladness; / But thereof come in the end despondency and madness."

At this point he spies the Leech-gatherer, old, poor, and infirm, in what seems a moment of significance: "Now, whether it were by peculiar grace, / A leading from above, a something given. . . ." A conversation with him impresses the poet with the old man's cheerful and dignified acceptance of his struggle:

> and when he ended,
> I could have laughed myself to scorn to find
> In that decrepit Man so firm a mind.
> "God," said I, "be my help and stay secure;
> I'll think of the Leech-gatherer on the lonely moor!"

As is "Summer Wish," "Resolution and Independence" is concerned with the poet's state of high expectation or high receptivity that can subject him to painful disappointment for which he is unprepared. The remedy, however, is simpler for Wordsworth's protagonist—resolution and independence. If the Leech-gatherer can manage, so can the poet, with the help of God. Bogan's poem reflects the increased knowledge of psychology and the further diminished religious faith of a later time. Hers is a "wish," not a resolution. She delves much deeper into her psyche than does Wordsworth and comes up with a more tentative answer. Her words are concentrated and referential; his are readily available to the reader. His anxieties for the future seem to be conventional—a dread of loneliness or grief or material want—while Bogan's fears have to do with the inner working of her mind. But are Wordsworth's concerns so conventional, really,

or do the lines about "fears and fancies thick" and "Dim sadness—
and blind thoughts, I knew not, nor could name" indicate more than
fits the conventional mold he builds around them in the lines that
follow? It also seems likely that "despondency and madness" result
from more than a genial, happy life that does not provide for tomorrow. Bogan is able to look more directly for, if not at, the nature of
her fears. For example, in another poem in *Dark Summer,* "Cassan-
dra," she treats the hazardous situation of the poet:

> To me, one silly task is like another.
> I bear the shambling tricks of lust and pride.
> This flesh will never give a child its mother,—
> Song, like a wing, tears through my breast, my side,
> And madness chooses out my voice again,
> Again. I am the chosen no hand saves:
> The shrieking heaven lifted over men,
> Not the dumb earth, wherein they set their graves.
>
>   (33)

In this poem there is a clearer cause-and-effect connection between
the vocation of the poet and the threat of madness.

Because of Bogan's ability to search within, "Summer Wish" is
also a more penetrating analysis of a crisis of maturity than is "Resolution and Independence."[31] It is her concern with the essence of
life, the meaning, that makes a difference as well in the use of the
dialogue form she borrows from Yeats's "Shepherd and Goatherd."
Yeats is concerned in his lament for Robert Gregory with tying tradition to the effort to console Lady Gregory for the death of her son.
He uses a classical form to dignify the mourning by connecting it
with great artists of the past, and a dialogue to express both the anguish felt for a lost young life and the philosophical consolation of
life's troubles missed by early death. The Shepherd of the valley presents the view of youth. It is he who has wished when he heard the
first cuckoo, and mourns Gregory as coming briefly and vanishing as
does the cuckoo. The Goatherd of the mountain, the view of age,
replies:

> You sing as always of the natural life,
> And I that made like music in my youth
> Hearing it now have sighed for that young man
> And certain lost companions of my own.

The Shepherd:

> They say that on your barren mountain ridge
> You have measured out the road that the soul treads
> When it has vanished from our natural eyes;
> That you have talked with apparitions.

The Goatherd affirms that he looks beyond nature for knowledge: "Indeed / My daily thoughts since the first stupor of youth / Have found the path my goats' feet cannot find." When the Shepherd asks the Goatherd to sing because "it may be that your thoughts have plucked / Some medicable herb to make our grief / Less bitter," the Goatherd replies, "They have brought me from that ridge / Seed-pods and flowers that are not all wild poppy," but, nonetheless, sings of death as stripping away the burden of life—both pain and joy—to a condition of happy childhood, "All knowledge lost in trance / Of sweeter ignorance." The poem concludes in a manner to tie the lament for Gregory to a future tradition as well as to the past: "To know the mountain and the valley have grieved / May be a quiet thought to wife and mother, / And children when they spring up shoulder-high."

Bogan's poem, though inspired by "Shepherd and Goatherd," is very different. In the first place, it is a much more personal poem because it deals with her own life rather than with an attempt to console another. Rather than with the significance of death it is concerned with the essence of life, with a means of living. Hope diminishes with the loss of youth in both poems, but in Bogan's the identification with nature remains rather than a moving away to the philosophical mountaintop. Age, in Yeats's poem, has lost faith with the "natural life" and looks beyond it for fulfillment. The poet in Bogan's poem (perhaps because Bogan was about twenty years younger at the time of writing her poem than Yeats was when writing his) is still seeking for life itself.

"Summer Wish" is a culmination of the poems of *Dark Summer* as well as the last poem in the volume. It is an attempt to dispel the darkness and to reorder the future. Images and feelings of poems throughout the book are tied together in "Summer Wish" with insight into their subconscious nature if not into their specific nature. As Sister Angela says of the poem, Bogan "confronts and extracts all

the bitterness and hurt of childhood, youth, and adult life."[32] Harold
Bloom considers it "the crisis and mid-point of her work." It is the
end of one season of Bogan's life and the beginning of another. Unfortunately, the summer of life was truly to be dark for Bogan, and
it would be eight years before her next volume of poetry would be
published.

Chapter Six
Short Stories

Depression

On December 26, 1929, while Louise Bogan and Raymond Holden were away, the house in Hillsdale, New York, burned along with their manuscripts and journals. A few days later, Bogan wrote Harriet Monroe a letter to explain the consequent delay in finishing a review for *Poetry* magazine and told her about the fire. It had been caused by the furnace through the negligence of the man left in charge. Everything was destroyed. Although covered by insurance, the house and their possessions could never be fully replaced. She said that the important thing, however, was that they were alive: "We are really quite well. Do not think us tragic figures."[1]

Despite her disavowal of tragedy, the fire was a loss that worsened an increasingly unhappy and ill period of Bogan's life. Her creativity was beginning to diminish because of anxiety, and the loss of her journals made it harder for her to recoup. Her marriage to Holden came to an end during this period, and old emotional insecurities compounded the present ones. She sought medical help and twice during these hard years had herself hospitalized.

In Amherst Library there is a journal begun in 1930 and ending with a note dated March 30, 1934, that records the anguish of those years. In one entry dated October 1930, Bogan carries on an imaginary conversation with her will and her imagination that in the past year "have slept a long sleep blinded." Her will urges her to try to write "in a style as hard as a brick" and to give up symbols. Her imagination argues that poetry does not come from the will alone, but from the language of dream, and in any event she cannot be other than what she is, a product of both will and imagination.[2]

In the same month, she received the *Poetry* magazine John Reed Memorial Prize for *Body of This Death, Dark Summer,* and poems published in *Poetry*. Her letter to Harriet Monroe acknowledging the award suggests that her creative depression was caused by lack of support for her work in the literary world. Beginning "I cannot think of

any recognition that has ever touched me so deeply," she explains
that she has been discouraged from writing in the past year by what
she feels to be subjective criticism from certain groups. She says:

> At the second or third meeting with a kind of subtle and refined cruelty, I
> abjured poetry. I no longer wished to say myself.
>   I tell you these reasons because your award has not only made them clear
> in my mind, but to a great extent has nullified them. I am refreshed, and
> hope to get out of this fog a sane and balanced person.—That the prize was
> given to my work in general delights me, because I have never been able to
> compete, in contests, or to write to order or on terms.[3]

The Themes of the Short Stories

The difficulties with poetry were far from over, however. Bogan
turned to prose, although still writing poetry; and the years 1931
through 1935 are the years during which most of her short stories
appeared in the *New Yorker*. (She had written stories earlier: "Keramik" was published in the *American Caravan* in 1927 and two short
prose pieces in the *New Republic* in 1928.) In addition to these published short stories, there are several unpublished ones at Amherst.[4]
All of Bogan's short stories, both published and unpublished, are
psychological studies that utilize a particular incident to illuminate
a mental state or an element of personality. They are tightly con-
structed and well-written for the most part. But the concern here is
not to judge their literary merit but to consider them for the aid they
give in understanding Bogan's poetry. The themes of the stories arise
from the same sources as the poetry, but during this period of emotional pain, prose was a relief from the direct emotional confrontation
of poetry.

"Keramik" is about a sophisticated old man who has a series of
love affairs with impressionable young women. Set in Europe, it concerns the old man's lack of feeling for the young women he is attentive to for a brief period and then drops:

> He had taught them all something and had learned nothing in return.
> There was always more to teach. They were all so much at sea, so stupid or
> so given to dreams. With each new lover their lives stopped or began. With
> him they were greedy, or chattering, or vain,—freer than a younger man
> could make them. They all had been so brief that they were perfectly,
> sharply outlined. They never thought themselves insecure, although tomor-
> row they were gone. All brief, save that one wise, quiet girl.[5]

After he drops this "quiet girl," she is quickly noticed by an attentive young man, about whom her emotions are mixed: "Something not her heart is beating,—something like pity, like revenge, in the middle of her body." The story ends with a description of the old man's remoteness: "the well of his old heart, cooler than women's wisdom, or passion, or chastity."

One of the short prose pieces published in the *New Republic*, "Art Embroidery," describes women in a department store sewing section as hiding the barrenness and pain of their lives in home decoration ("Now they have stitches for tomorrow, put in to clothe the hours. They have time").[6] The embroidery hides the women's pain in the form of design. The women, as in "Keramik," are viewed as dependents, as victims. A later story, "The Last Tear," published in the *New Yorker* in 1933, has an apparently single mother (widowed or divorced, that is) traveling in Europe with her daughter. She has given her daughter cultural advantages, although money is scarce, and now the daughter spends time and money frivolously with fashionable friends, leaving the mother lonely and regretting that her daughter's education was not geared more closely to her own:

> She wished, as the rum warmed her cold, tight throat, that she had always been alone, or that she never had allowed Claire to learn to read and write, let alone swim, ride, and weave. Then she might have had a happy life. She would not have needed Trieste beer or medicinal cognac or cigarettes or *cachets*. She would have needed nothing but the affection, the comfort, the companionship derived from a truly dutiful, uninstructed child. She and this other Claire could have led a quiet life somewhere under a fig tree and vine in a garden. She herself would have taught Claire to knit, to strum on the piano, to cook, to sing, to sew.[7]

The tone indicates that it is the loneliness rather than the daughter's education that is regretted, the loss of a companionship she had counted on.

During the thirties, when Bogan was writing many stories, there were several treating some aspect of relationships between men and women, and the aspect was always a negative one. In "Sabbatical Summer" (1931), a young English teacher comes to New York from Cleveland.[8] He considers himself an artist, not a bourgeois, and falls in love with an artistic Bohemian girl who lives in the Village. He plans to ask her to marry him until he runs into "an extremely nice" friend of his sister's from Cleveland and is suddenly revolted by his unconventional girl friend whom he does not introduce to his sister's friend.

An empty marriage is the subject of "A Speakeasy Life" (1931).[9] A wife of several years believes that her husband is bored and wants a gayer life, when actually—as she discovers when a friend comes to town—it is she who wants the other life. In the delineations of the husband and wife, little sympathy or understanding between them is shown.

The protagonist of "Summer Day," unpublished,[10] is a woman who is hurt by a male friend suddenly saying goodbye in the middle of the afternoon. She had wanted to go to a museum, but he feels he must get back to his office. He had arrived at her place at eleven-thirty in the morning, and they had listened to the records he had come for and then gone out to lunch. Now she feels that she has tired him; she resents her hurt when the outing was his idea in the first place, and morning had been a bad time for her to socialize. She goes back over the hours in a self-critical but resentful way and feels that he blames her for his bad conscience in losing time from work. This brief synopsis overly simplifies the story whose thrust is the ready self-concern of the man and the eagerness to please of the woman.

Another unpublished story, "Saturday Night Minimum," carries on the typescript the address where Bogan lived from October 1935 to March 1936; so it presumably was written during this time.[11] The couple in this case is talking and drinking in a nightclub. That is, the man is talking and the woman listening. But between one show and another, the "romance" ends without the man's being aware of it. The process of projecting a self-pleasing image on the other person can change into an unpleasant one without having anything to do with who the romanticized person really is. There is a mixed feeling of rejection and hostility in the tone of the story, and it is not completely clear who is really rejecting whom. As in "Keramik," there is role playing accompanied by resentment. The story ends: "On Saturday nights there was a minimum charge attached to the drinks."

In "Whatever It Is," dated in script "1936 (Spring)" and unpublished,[12] the narrator says in the opening paragraph that the nature of the human heart appears to have changed over time. As illustration and prompter of the remark, she tells of an incident in which a handsome man of her acquaintance, presumably paying discreet attention to an attractive married friend, Evelyn (at least, Evelyn believes so), is discovered to be in love with a friend of the friend, Margaret, an academic considered harmless and boring by the usually jealous, more attractive Evelyn. Margaret is described—with that ambivalent feeling toward women often found in Bogan—as having "that semi-learned look, the nearest a woman can get to the really learned look found on male academic faces." The narrator reflects on the time Evelyn has spent at the beauty parlor trying to create an image that would bring her the admiration she wants and thinks how in error one can be in assessing the qualities that will arouse human passion. The conventional notions of attractiveness are not operating in what she refers to as "the illusory world."

Social Illusion

The "illusory world" is found in society at large, as well as in men/women relationships, in "Sunday at Five" (1931)[13] and in "Conversation Piece" (1933).[14] In "Sunday at Five" a woman at a cocktail party is suddenly overcome with the artificiality of the scene and feels suffocated and that she "must get out of here," because otherwise

underneath a howling, growling, yowling rage—unaccountable, and usually in check—[she] would throw the trick cigarette-lighter against the glass of the banal modern print, snatch the curtains from under the tasteful valance boards, shatter the horrid vase full of affected arum lilies, twist strings of beads tightly around politely arched necks, muffle the bright new tune on the phonograph, shout down the four differing, acquired English accents, curse, swear, yell, and scream, and wipe and wipe and wipe (here she began to repeat herself, in her fury, like a needle stuck in one groove of a record) and wipe from the face of Amy, and from the faces of all her friends and all the strangers, the smile wherein friendship, sympathy, indeed any natural human feeling, lay horribly embalmed.

In actuality, she accepts another drink offered by the young man who is talking to her.

In "Conversation Piece" one couple visits another in a New York apartment. The hosts are gracious and charming, but underneath a facade of genteel interests, especially an interest in Mozart's music, the conversation essentially becomes malicious gossip about mutual acquaintances.

Another form of social illusion, that of the young person who romanticizes the life of an older person, is the subject of "Letdown."[15]

A thirteen-year-old idolizes her sixty-year-old art teacher who represents a grander world:

Personal distinction, in those days, to me meant undoubted nobility of soul.
Distinguished physical traits went right through to the back, as it were,
indelibly staining mind and spirit. And Miss Cooper, being stamped all
over with the color and designs of art as well as by the traits of gentility,
made double claims upon my respect and imagination.

After two years of seeing Miss Cooper "at a continual point of perfection . . . beyond simple human needs," the young girl becomes
crushingly disillusioned to see her one day "standing with a greasy
paper bag in one hand and a half-eaten doughnut in the other." The
image shatters the young girl's created "world of romantic notions."
There is no pity for the old woman, only pity for herself and "for
dignity and gentility soiled and broken." The narrator comments,
"At fifteen and for a long time thereafter, it is a monstrous thing,
the heart."

Not a short story, but in the words of the piece itself, "a short
speech to take leave," "To Take Leave" begins, "Now, look here, my
fine pair, widely known as Sorrow and Romantic Attachment, I have
entertained the thought of you over a long period of years," and proceeds to enumerate the ways in which they have constantly shaped
her life. But now they have become much less attractive: "The intense pleasures of anxiety, as time passes, attract me less and less."
In a satirical tone, she bids them good-bye.[16]

Mirrors

The intensity of perception and feeling leading to youthful romanticism and, conversely, to mature despair is best described in "With
Mirrors," dated "1937?" and also unpublished.[17] The words that describe the acute awareness of the poet are vividly descriptive:

Those were the days when there were few other things that I did not hear
or see. My hearing continually went up and down the streets with the
traffic; my sight was continually determined to master everything around it.
Within walls, I saw everything, actively, from baseboard to ceiling; faced
with a scene in nature I accomplished prodigious visual feats with fore-
ground, background, and middle distance. I had a dreadful habit of plung-
ing into casual faces, of reading all the signs, of attempting to see around

corners, of trying to cope with the full blaze of noonday and complete midnight darkness.

But the time came when the intensity was a burden, and she made a conscious effort to resist. However, when the narrator relaxed her intense observation, appearances seemed unreal; she apprehended matters with "so much detachment that they became a little queer." One day she notices how many mirrors and polished surfaces there are in the city and how unaffected people are by their reflections in them. She becomes impressed over a period of time with the situation:

One extraordinary underground room had walls rising to a great height, entirely coated with black mirror which greatly resembled the ice peculiar to the ninth circle of Dante's hell. In this room many persons sat smoking cigarettes, as if unaware of their surroundings.

In the end, the thought occurs to her "how mirrors are sometimes placed before lonely animals to give them the illusion of companionship. But that was a far too relaxed thought, and I put it out of my mind. . . ."

Mirrors and their reflections are significant in Bogan's work. In "The Cupola," "Old Countryside," and "The Flume" there are mirrors that bring nature indoors. "Long gilded mirrors gaze" in another poem, "Hypocrite Swift." Bogan indicates in a letter written on February 14, 1933, to Morton Zabel that she has experienced such a mirrored room as is described in "With Mirrors":

That review (ten books polished off in 1100 words) always disaffects me thoroughly, so that I have to take long ferry rides to Hoboken, long walks all over town, and long drinks of beer at four in the afternoon (alone, in Luchow's, with the reflection of my self going up into infinity in the long funereal mirrors).[18]

The black mirrors turn up again in an unpublished short story, "Not Love, but Ardor," in a line of dialogue: " 'People must be lulled,' she said. 'Even reflected in black mirrors, a hundred feet below the street, people must be lulled.' "[19] The patient in "Hydrotherapy," a short story, reacts to a mirror: "The long mirror again faced her, but she did not look into it. She had taken a vow against mirrors."[20] Reflections are a remove from reality, or reality in a

strange context, as life can seem to one who constantly seeks more
than is readily apparent or at hand.

Deadness of Feeling

The feeling of being intensely alive occurs briefly only to be con-
sumed by the necessary business of life in "The Short Life of
Emily."[21] A forty-year-old, on her way to her lawyer's office—walking because she has taken the wrong elevated train to the wrong
stop—suddenly realizes that she is alive. She has a sharp realization
of the minutiae of the moment. She becomes aware of the people
around her as events in her life and the scenes through which she is
passing as scenes in her life: "This is Emily. This is herself. This is
she." But upon arriving on the fifth floor of her lawyer's building,

something happens to her conviction of existence. The car door slams, and
she is alone. Almost instantly, she forgets that she lives, that she breathes,
that she has being—as is only natural, as we, too, in her place would forget.
This is the fifth floor: that is all, suddenly, that she can really take in, or
remember.

Another story, "Zest," published in 1931, takes a harsher view of
the nature of the vital force.[22] Seeking to escape a "nervous state," a
woman decides to test the advice of a book to "Love someone or
something, take interest in things outside yourself, and cultivate
zest." She can't think of a feeling of love for another that she has that
is strong enough to help her; so she decides to get out of herself and
feel zest. She goes out to the street and eventually takes a ride on a
streetcar, noticing buildings and people. But, except for the News
Building with the chain of thought it begins about the immensity of
mass communication, nothing really stirs zest until she suddenly
thinks of stopping for lunch. During the whole sequence of events,
a bit of gossip that she has heard keeps popping up in her mind
("Charles' wife was reported to have left him after having taken up
with a mere boy"), and now when she is in a good restaurant, antic-
ipating lunch, she becomes very excited at the sight of a telephone.
The anticipation of calling a friend, Lucy, who will know the details
of the gossip gives zest to her whole day. As a reference to calling
Lucy earlier in the story has been designated falling back upon usual
habits, it is to be wondered if there is confusion about the cause of
the nervous state, if a return to zest is brought about by glee in gossip, or if there is a little vindictiveness involved. Written in the

months after Bogan's own period of depression in early 1931, the story seems to foreshadow the view of the poem "At a Party" with its concluding lines:

> Step forth, then, malice, wisdom's guide,
> And enmity, that may save us all.[23]

Emotional Illness

Bogan wrote directly about the process of recovering from an emotional breakdown and the part hating or loving plays in that process in an article, "Coming Out," for the *New Yorker* in 1933. She wrote that a person goes in ("Your nervous system yawns before you like the entrance to the pit and you are going in") when he is convinced that all the world is happy and sound except himself and comes out when, either by hating or loving, he receives a clear enough view of his fellows to make him see that he is no more abnormal nor unhappy than they.[24]

The actual process of hospital recovery is treated in two short stories, "Hydrotherapy," published in 1931, and "The Long Walk," written about 1935 and unpublished (the typescript has written on it in script "Winter [1934–1935]").[25] "Hydrotherapy" takes the protagonist, a young woman with a "tired psyche," through a treatment of hot steam and hot and cold water, describing the experience and her feelings from her point of view. It is sensitive to both the frightening and curative aspects of institutional health care and ends on a gentle note:

She was rubbed dry. And suddenly, for a little moment, for a fraction of a clock-tick as she leaned against the wall to balance herself while she put her feet into her slippers, she felt very strange. Just for a split second, as she caught the eye of the fat nurse who winked, she stopped suffering. (19)

"The Long Walk" involves a group of women in an institution who are taken on a walk every afternoon at four o'clock. It recounts their reactions to getting outdoors and being with one another, and seeing the "houses of the town" from outside; it tells of their struggles with their own illnesses:

The long hospital building stood before them, and soon they would have tea.
They had gone such a short distance, but no matter how often they took

that journey, they were puzzled again that this should be the end of it; that wherever they had been, they should be made to come back here. (6)

Relationship to Poetry

Whether concerned with illness, relationships, or the meaning of living, the essence of Bogan's prose writing is always psychological—how someone or some people feel about a particular situation or condition. The meanings are not always clear-cut, but involve ambiguous reactions and impulses. The need for but difficulty in achieving human love is a major concern, given societal and personal blindness and perversity. The oppressiveness of mutability and the cruel, unknowable nature of the universe that defeat aspiration underlie all the writings. These themes go beyond the personal, beyond Bogan herself.

That many of her own psychic concerns furnished material for the stories is apparent from the autobiographical data in her letters, and it is for this reason that the prose provides insight into the poetry.[26] In looking for the meanings behind the symbols of Bogan's poetry, however, the most important prose sources are "Journey Around My Room" and "Dove and Serpent," the autobiographical writings discussed in relation to "Medusa."

Chapter Seven
The Sleeping Fury

Return to Poetry

Writing short stories was not to be a lifetime interest for Bogan because she was always happier with poetry, feeling that it alone expressed what she had to say. In 1925 she had told Ruth Benedict in a letter that "prose is so terribly unsatisfactory. Everything in it could be said in any number of ways. While a poem is itself, inevitably, unerringly."[1] She wrote poetry when she could during this time of anxiety and, encouraged by Harriet Monroe to apply for a Guggenheim Fellowship in creative writing, did so, although reluctantly, as she explained to Monroe:

> I remembered our talk of last winter and finally put aside my fears of failure and my sin of pride. It is not in my nature to apply, to ask for. . . . I applied because I sincerely believe, now, that there's some poetry left in what the mystics would call my soul and the psychologists my subconscious. It will come out, Guggenheim or no. The fellowship would amplify and enrich some aspects of it.[2]

Awarded the fellowship, Bogan made plans to sail in April for Italy.[3] But Europe apparently did not cure her lack of productivity. She spent two months in Italy and went on to France, where she wrote Monroe, "And now I shall begin to work. . . . I'll send you poems when they are written."[4] However, she does not seem to have sent any during the summer. Moreover, upon her return to New York at the end of the summer, she and Raymond Holden separated. By the following January (1934), she felt herself sufficiently emotionally ill to enter a hospital, "nervously prostrated, having lost the power to take 'an objective view,' to make 'clear-cut decisions,' " as she put it.[5]

She was in the hospital for several months, but she did make progress in overcoming her inability to work. While there, she started "Laura Dailey's Story," the autobiographical work mentioned earlier.

She grew well and began to write more freely. By August, having been back home all summer, she was writing Edmund Wilson, "I write and write—more than I've done in years."[6] Her biggest battle with what she called her "warring elements" was being won during these months, and she became less subject to old fears.[7] Her letters indicate that for the rest of her life she considered this time to be a turning point, a time when her mature personality began to emerge (in a letter to May Sarton, for example, in 1954 she referred to her "general making over of the emotional personality [in 1933]").[8]

When it came time to put together the poems for *The Sleeping Fury*, published early in 1937, Bogan chose for the title page the lines from "Der Schauende" ("The Spectator") from *Buch der Bilder* (*Picture Book*), by Rainer Maria Rilke:

> Wie ist das klein, womit wir ringen;
> was mit uns ringt, wie ist das gross. . . .[9]
>
> (How small is that with which we struggle;
> how great is that which struggles with us. . . .)

Bogan had begun to read Rilke in 1935. She wrote John Hall Wheelock on July 1 of that year:

> And I've just discovered Rilke. Why did you never tell me about Rilke? My God, the man's wonderful. Perhaps, sometime this summer, you will come down, in the late afternoon, and I'll provide some rye, and you can help me with some of the harder verses in the *Neue Gedichte*. My German is still so poor.[10]

She was to continue to read and to translate Rilke for years to come.[11] From this time forward, all her collections of poems carried the Rilke lines on the title page.

The Long View

The lines express the underlying philosophy of the poems of *The Sleeping Fury*, which were written during this crucial time in Bogan's life and work. She dedicated the volume, "in gratitude," to her long-time friend, Edmund Wilson, whose companionship seems to have been particularly supportive during these years. His intellectual interests complemented hers, and he encouraged her when she needed

it. The summer of 1934, a few months after a period of hospitalization, she wrote Morton Zabel:

Then E. Wilson invited me down here. In New York the one bright spot
in my horrid early summer had been our German evening. We got together
two nights a week and read Heine, aided by two dictionaries.[12]

Such mental activity apparently was both healing and essential to Bogan. She was always almost driven by the need to understand. In
1933 she had said, "Everyone is more or less miserable everywhere,
and the one thing to remember is that intellectual curiosity and the
life of the mind are man's hope, and let it go at that."[13] It took seven
years of trying to understand her own direction and to evolve to emotional health to complete the poems of *The Sleeping Fury*.

Bogan's flippant description of the volume in a letter of 1936 ob-
scures the real struggle that went into it. Characteristically, she jokes
about what is painfully personal:

The S. F. is now in sections: four of them. It rises and falls, from despair,
to exaltation, and back again: Bogan in cothurnus [a shoe worn by classical
tragic actors] and Bogan in flat heels. . . .
    Seriously, the poems shape up pretty well. The 1930–1933 period—de-
spair, neurosis and alcoholism—is set off by itself, ending with "Hypocrite
Swift." Then there is the period of further despair, edged in upon by the
period of Beautiful Males (ending with "Man Alone"). Then the spiritual
side begins, with a few rumbles from the sensual bassoons and the mystic
fiddles. All ends on a note of calm: me and the landscape clasped in each
other's arms.[14]

Before the final shape of *The Sleeping Fury*, Bogan had listed some
translations to be included. A manuscript worksheet lists Baudelaire
and Lucretius, and a letter written apparently later mentions "Some
renderings, of Lucretius and, perhaps, Rilke." That this plan was
abandoned was probably due to the number of her own poems that
she finally included.[15]

The impersonality of the long view that Bogan found apt in Rilke's
lines often exacted the price of loss of expectation and enthusiasm,
unfortunately. Lyric poetry is particularly expressive of the height-
ened feelings of youth; when the experiences of maturity alter the
feelings, the bases of the poetry shift. It is this problem of shifting
bases that the poems of part 1 of *The Sleeping Fury* are concerned with.

"Homunculus," the third poem in this part, portrays a "ruse" by which the mind goes on, or the life force goes on, when the emotional reasons change. In the article written in 1923, "The Springs of Poetry," Bogan had described what happens when a poet flinches from the strong, motivating feeling behind the poem: "He writes a poem at third, fourth, or fifth hand, bred out of some delicate fantastic ruse of the brain."[16] "Homunculus" expresses the dissatisfaction such an attempt brings:

> O see what I have made!
> A delicate precious ruse
> By which death is betrayed
> And all time given use.
>
> See this fine body, joined
> More cleanly than a thorn.
> What man, though lusty-loined,
> What woman from woman born,
>
> Shaped a slight thing, so strong,
> Or a wise thing, so young?
> This mouth will yet know song
> And words move on this tongue.
>
> It lacks but life: some scent,
> Some kernel of hot endeavor,
> Some dust of dead content
> Will make it live forever.[17]

"It lacks but life" is the emotional key to the seven poems of this first part. "Song" ("It is not now I learn"), the beginning poem, is a musical lyric that represents a human emotional cycle in images of nature. In maturity, the promise that spring gives of green grass and leaves has the knowledge of the scythe and the burned stubble. The heart, "the stone," defensively narrows "to the wind" of disappointment. That a poem which "turns the heart away" should be musical serves to emphasize the lost feeling of youthful lyricism. The form is there of happier times, but the words modify its meaning. A stronger statement of the fear of intensity is "Henceforth, from the Mind" in which emotion is placed at a safe remove like the sound of the ocean in a conch shell, "A smothered sound that sleeps/Long lost within lost deeps."

The Distancing of Form

What poetry means to Bogan, what form says that she cannot otherwise say, is illuminated by "Single Sonnet." The emotion that she cannot personally afford, "the weight in the heart that breathes, but cannot move," is safely expressed in a traditional form, a sonnet that removes it to the province of society: "Staunch meter, great song, it is yours, at length. . . ." The typescript says "Written in Cromwell Hall (a sanitarium), Connecticut, May, 1931":[18]

> Now, you great stanza, you heroic mould,
> Bend to my will, for I must give you love:
> The weight in the heart that breathes, but cannot move,
> Which to endure flesh only makes so bold.
>
> Take up, take up, as it were lead or gold
> The burden; test the dreadful mass thereof.
> No stone, slate, metal under or above
> Earth, is so ponderous, so dull, so cold.
>
> Too long as ocean bed bears up the ocean,
> As earth's core bears the earth, have I borne this;
> Too long have lovers, bending for their kiss,
> Felt bitter force cohering without motion.
>
> Staunch meter, great song, it is yours, at length,
> To prove how stronger you are than my strength.
>
> (66)

A more direct, more bitter, statement of futility is the poem that follows "Single Sonnet." Bogan called it "a fine, frightfully angry, terrifically compressed poem,"[19] and explained that she thought it a good poem "because, on a second reading, it sounded like something I had never seen before, and I always take that as a sign that the vulgar upper consciousness had nothing to do with it."[20] Who "the dead" mentioned in the poem are, I do not know. Both her first husband, Alexander, and her brother were dead at this time, but I believe that Bogan is not referring to dead personalities but to the force of those who went before, traditional ways of thinking and doing that shape the present. She commented in 1936 that on one occasion she had thought, "There will be a race that will go up this street singing, and, perhaps, leading beautiful animals, garlanded with roses, and

each one wise and noble in his heart, but I knew it wouldn't be produced by our age, or even by the means thrown up by our age. And
a lot of blood will have to flow before it comes, and lots of air will
need to be let into the generations before it."[21] Even more forceful
than tradition, perhaps, is the archetypal pattern of repeated experiences in the generations. Bogan once wrote a poem (unpublished)
called "Hell" in which the dead sit in rows and mockingly watch a
performance, "an eternal vaudeville," of the living.[22] Because Bogan
considered calling "Exhortation" "All Souls' Eve," it is helpful to
bear in mind this view of the dead when reading "Exhortation" with
its lines "It is the dead we live among,/The dead given motion, and
a tongue."[23]

The next to last poem of this section, "Hypocrite Swift," was written while Bogan was recovering from a period of emotional illness in
1931. The manuscript has a subtitle, "After Reading Swift's Journal
to Stella,"[24] and Bogan wrote Edmund Wilson from the Connecticut
sanitarium: "I'm glad you liked the Swift poem. The *Journal to Stella*
wrung my heart. The passion is so real, so imperfectly dissembled,
and the wit is such a strange mixture of roughness and elegance."[25]
She had begun the poem as an exercise but found that it turned into
a real poem. This discovery she credited with hastening her return to
health.[26] It is not surprising that Bogan would respond to Swift's
confused feelings at this time when for her, too, "Venus, the Muses
stare above the maze./Now sleep" (69).

Mixed Feelings

After returning home, Bogan wrote Harriet Monroe:

I am much better, although by no means completely well. Several mechanisms have broken down and a strange new period has set in, in my heart
and mind. I feel at once renewed and disinherited. Different people say different things. My doctor insists that I love; Robert Frost, whom we saw
recently, recommends fear and hatred. But I have lost faith in universal panaceas—work is the one thing in which I really believe.[27]

It must have been in much this frame of mind that "At a Party,"
mentioned in the previous chapter, was written.

During the period when these poems were being written, three
other poems were printed in the *New Yorker* which Bogan chose not
to collect—"For an Old Dance," "The Engine," and "Gift." "For an

Old Dance" (1930) is slight verse on a *carpe diem* theme of "We shall grow old" and "All loves abate."[28] It is unsuccessful as light verse because of a certain awkwardness of feeling and expression. Underneath, the feeling is not really light. "The Engine" (1931) is more successful, though not light, but its metaphor of the heart/engine that runs the body regardless of the experience of personality and mind is reminiscent of the first two stanzas of "Fifteenth Farewell" without being as well developed.[29] In contrast to these two poems, and in contrast to the collected poems just discussed, "Gift" (1932) is a simple love song that indicates that Bogan was capable of following her doctor's advice to love as well as Frost's to hate. Bogan probably considered it too simple to collect or too personal.[30]

The Struggle for Perspective

Between the times of writing of the poems of part 1 and part 2 of *The Sleeping Fury* were Bogan's summer in Europe on a Guggenheim Fellowship (1933), her separation from her husband, and her second hospitalization for emotional illness in late 1933 or the early part of 1934. There are five poems in part 2, and they all seem to have been written after her recovery in 1934.[31] They reflect overall a discouragement with life's prospects, although "Italian Morning" seeks to put personal mortality in philosophical perspective.

The first, "To Wine," is dismal in its sense of helplessness against anxiety and grief. The neurotic concern with infidelity and reassurance mars the first stanza, as the sense of cynicism—that wine can provide "all that is worth grief"—mars the entire poem. The adjectives "ignorant and cruel" apply, I think, to life as well as to wine in the poem's meaning. Perhaps the dead person is Bogan's first husband and, therefore, a source of forever unresolved conflict; or perhaps it is her brother who was killed in World War I. It is not necessary, of course, for the reference to be to personal reality, but it seems to me that Bogan's other poetry indicates that she wrote from her own feelings.

"Poem in Prose," "Short Summary," and "Man Alone" all treat an aspect of romantic love—transitory romantic love, that is. None of the poems indicates a belief in permanence. "Poem in Prose" doesn't ring true, in my opinion; the meaning is unconsciously dishonest. "Virtue" and "desperate esteem" are confused, and one gets the feeling of a fictional creation of intensity. The imagery of the third and fourth lines carries the weight of the poem: "the true inheritors of love, / The bearers; their strong hair moulded to their foreheads as though by the pressure of hands" (p. 72). "Short Summary" is much better. It delicately balances season and time of day with the hope of a beginning relationship but the lateness of life or opportunity. It is musical and unified in feeling and thought, despite the disclaimer of the first sentence: "Listen but once to the words written out by my hand / In the long line fit only for giving ease / To the tiresome heart." That kind of long line I found in "Poem in Prose" but not in "Short Summary." A picture of egocentrism that seeks a reflection of self in others, "Man Alone" is a caustic poem of short, fast-moving lines which builds to the climactic last stanza in which even the lover is a stranger to him who is infatuated with only himself. The image of the man is similar to that of the man in the short story, "Saturday Night Minimum."

Among these poems is "Italian Morning," more representative of Bogan's best work than the other four. Bogan thought so, too, and called it "the best poem I have done in years."[32] The feeling of cyclic change, of mutability, is juxtaposed throughout to the feeling of destiny and eternity, from the transience of the visitor to the permanence of the marble arch, the brevity of the magnolia blossom to the endurance of the painted flower, and from the sense of individual loss of the first stanza to the apprehension of a larger permanence:

> Half circle's come before we know.
> Full in the falling arc, we hear
> Our heel give earth a lonely blow.
> We place the hour and name the year.
>
> High in a room long since designed
> For our late visit under night,
> We sleep: we wake to watch the lined
> Wave take strange walls with counterfeit light.
>
> The big magnolia, like a hand,
> Repeats our flesh. (O bred to love,
> Gathered to silence!) In a land
> Thus garnished, there is time enough
>
> To pace the rooms where painted swags
> Of fruit and flower in pride depend,
> Stayed as we are not. The hour wags
> Deliberate, and great arches bend

In long perspective past our eye.

Mutable body, and brief name,
Confront, against an early sky,
This marble herb, and this stone flame.   (74)

Growth and Maturity

Part 3 continues the philosophic tenor of "Italian Morning" and contains the title poem, "The Sleeping Fury." This last poem, together with "Putting to Sea" (in part 4), Bogan called the nucleus of the book, although she did not write these poems until after her first plans for the volume were made. It was a time of growth, and she was writing more poems than usual during this period as she adjusted to the changing viewpoints coincident with her return to health. Not surprisingly, she did not finish, nor approve of, all of them. Her papers at Amherst contain poems and parts of poems from this period that were never published, but they indicate that she was struggling to find fit expression. Her crossed-out lines and revisions show her concern with form and authentic meaning. As she told her editor, John Hall Wheelock, in response to a request for a blurb about *The Sleeping Fury* (as poetry critic for the *New Yorker,* she had written many of the short critiques of new books called blurbs):

Can't someone else write the blurbs? I have to write so many on other people that I can't really bear to write one about myself. Whoever does it might try to make the point, mildly, that I care, really truly care, about the actual *writing* in a poem. That I have given some thought to the effects of tension, sonority, etc., that *language* can produce. That I consider, with Gautier: (here read his *L'Art* through), etc., etc. I also think that our unconscious (Uncs., in Freud's charming phraseology) knows more about us than we know about it.[33]

Théophile Gautier, a nineteenth-century French poet, had set forth his views of what art should be in his poem "L'Art." A paraphrase is as follows: Beautiful art—poetry, sculpture, painting—results from obdurate material that resists the work of the artist. Without using false constraints, the artist should discipline himself to avoid the easy rhythm, the soft clay, the watercolor, and to work with the enduring idea (without dogmas of politics or religion), the hard marble, bronze, or agate, and the oven-baked enamel. Only strong art is eternal; it survives the city, the emperor, and the gods themselves. Sovereign verses remain stronger than cannons. The artist should sculpt, file, chisel that his fragile dream may be fixed in the enduring block of his material.

In short, Gautier believed in the beauty of form that comes from form's ability to express the truth. But such form is not easily nor casually attained. The poet must sculpt from the unyielding language as the sculptor does from the hardest marble to bring forth the quintessential meaning. That Bogan shared this ideal, that she truly cared about the actual writing, is very evident in these poems. Words express through denotation or connotation, through the appeal of sound and rhythm, the meaning that strives always to rise above dogma or the merely personal. In addition, her opinion that the unconscious knows more about us than we know about it is evident in the reliance upon symbols and images to carry latent meaning in the poems of *The Sleeping Fury*. The unconscious, as manifested in symbols, was to remain the dominant force behind Bogan's poetry.

Bogan's tendency closely to criticize her work can be seen in connection with a poem, "The Lie." "Baroque Comment," "Roman Fountain," and "The Lie" were apparently written at about the same time. At least, all three are discussed by Bogan as being in process in the same letter to Rolfe Humphries.[34] "The Lie," which she included in the letter, was written in anger, she said, as she discussed the poem at length—its faults and its good points. It begins:

> First met when I was young;
> Within the sliding eye,
> Upon the sidling tongue,
> I knew the lie.[35]

The faults must have overpowered the good for her because she never published the poem. Of course, she was not completely pleased with "Roman Fountain," either; and she did publish that. In the long run, the tone of "The Lie" may have bothered her, although there were other problems with the poem. She wrote Humphries: "The third stanza begins to get too noble for anything, and that's bad, I suppose. As a matter of fact, I was a nervous, frightened kind of brat, with no particular claim to truthful bones, but I did hate to have my mother lie to me, but all kids do." The tone is the main fault, I believe. The subject of truth is an important concern, but the poem treats it shallowly and childishly.

Bogan may have satisfied her desire to treat the subject, if not in that poem, then by placing the lie among the destructive forces in "Baroque Comment" ("Coincident with the lie . . ."). The original manuscript of "Baroque Comment" does not mention the lie.[36] By including it in the company of "anger, lust, oppression and death in many forms," the nature of its harm is made clear as well, of course, as moving the concern beyond a personal one. The anger of the other poem is gone in the balance in "Baroque Comment" of chaos and art, of ignorance and knowledge, and of destruction and love. Rather than outrage, there is wonder at human attainment in spite of all.

"Roman Fountain," which Bogan called "minor, all save the first stanza" because "It should be all fountain, and no Louise looking at it," would not to my way of thinking be as forceful without "Louise looking at it." It concerns the poet's feelings primarily and the fountain itself—artistic creativity itself—secondarily. The fountain and the "air of summer" serve to parallel her emotional state and her joy in creativity. Images are "beat[en]" out, as is bronze, to capture and shape the natural elements to form the poem, or the spout of water.

> Up from the bronze, I saw
> Water without a flaw
> Rush to its rest in air,
> Reach to its rest, and fall.
>
> Bronze of the blackest shade,
> An element man-made,
> Shaping upright the bare
> Clear gouts of water in air.
>
> O, as with arm and hammer,
> Still it is good to strive
> To beat out the image whole,
> To echo the shout and stammer
> When full-gushed waters, alive,
> Strike on the fountain's bowl
> After the air of summer.
>
> (80)

One poem in part 3 was not written at the same time as the others. "To My Brother, Killed: Haumont Wood: October 1918" was found, along with another poem, "Hidden," by Rolfe Humphries in

his previous letters from Bogan. After he sent them to her, they were
published in the *New Yorker*.[37] She said that they were written "years
ago," but the manuscript of "Hidden" has "1932?" written on the
bottom, probably added later.[38] While the poem "Hidden" agrees in
publication form with the manuscript, "To My Brother" has a few
changes from the original that indicate Bogan's continuing move
away from anything she saw as romantic in form and toward a more
tempered outlook. She dropped the remnants of "poetic" language—
"you" in the first two lines was "thou" in the original. In the last
line, "peace" was in the original "flesh," expressing a more bitter
loss. As in "Italian Morning" and "Baroque Comment," human mortality is placed in the perspective of universal time and the individual
nature in the perspective of all humanity.

The other poem found by Humphries, "Hidden," has stanzas of
three lines with the second line of each much longer than the first
and third lines, creating, with the alternation of short, fast lines and
longer, slower-moving lines a sense of interior argument. The argument, itself, of the risk of achievement, Bogan may have seen later
as deriving too strictly from her own experience. Or, perhaps, she no
longer felt the same way. From the beginning lines—

> I thought to make
> The smallest possible compass for loveliness
> For safety's sake;

—the argument moves to the concluding stanzas:

> What shall I do?
> It cannot be small, so that any casual arrow
> May rive it in two.
>
> Beyond all size,
> Secret and huge, I shall mount it over the world,
> Before the bolt flies.

Two poems that were not printed but written during this time of
emotional readjustment are in the Bogan papers in typescript.[39] They
illustrate the struggle to overcome loss and fear and to obtain objectivity, but they also illustrate the pain causing the struggle. "We
Might Have Striven Years" is the more personal of the two, dealing
with a particular relationship that seems to have attained a level of

quiet acceptance. It welcomes the lack of intense involvement. The other, "When at Last" (printed since in *Journey Around My Room,* p. 68), is not particular but general in seeking an approach to life that rises above personal feeling. It was in 1935 that Bogan began to read Rilke, and he possibly influenced the thought behind the third and fourth lines: "[When at last we can] hum over to ourselves the tune made by the massed instruments / As the shell hums the sea." Certainly, this poem states the goal of Bogan's effort to understand her anxieties and motivations in this time of coming to terms with both childhood and adult feelings. Her strongest poems in this volume arise from the turbulence of this process.

"The Sleeping Fury"

It is no wonder that she termed the title poem central to the volume. "The Sleeping Fury," like "Medusa," deals with the complex of subconscious preoccupations stemming from early years, but with a dawning adult understanding that mitigates their power. Introducing the poem on a recording of her readings, she remarked only that she had seen such a sleeping Fury on a bas-relief in a museum.[40] Characteristically, she left it for the poem to say what the image had suggested to her.

It would be helpful for the reader of the poem, however, to remember that the Furies were creatures of Greek mythology who punished individuals for sins against family or group by tormenting them to the point of madness. Although versions vary, there were usually three Furies, representing anger (Alecto), jealousy (Megaera), and vengeance (Tisiphone). The primary characteristic of the idea of the Furies is that they dealt through the mind with crimes against important relationships. Bogan calls this Fury "avenger" in the fourth stanza, but a manuscript version also has "Megaera" written at the top of the page, indicating that her Fury was avenging jealousy.[41] The Fury, with its serpent-like hair (or serpents intertwined in the hair) recalls the Medusa image and is similarly personified as a woman. The Furies carried torches and scourges and were relentless. Bogan's painful relationship with her mother is unavoidably brought to mind, as is the question of whether Bogan's adult problems with jealousy were tied to that early situation. In any case, the self-destructive nature of any unresolved guilt/hate/love complex is recreated. In another manuscript version of the poem, the nature is made explicit in the line: "You, this scorner, this sister/Driving insane, because your purpose was hidden." The immense emotional power of childhood impressions felt but not understood as well as the dissipation of that power if the impressions are brought to the light of adult understanding are the subjects of this important poem.

The process of writing the poem was one of several stages, as the worksheets at Amherst show. There is a prose version, too—a one-page description that begins, "It was so loved, so feared, but now it lies in a symbol before us, fixed and asleep." All the other versions are in verse, as Bogan works her way through to the final form. The central theme remains the same, as do many of the images, indicating the strength of the initial impression.

When "The Sleeping Fury" was first published in *Poetry* in December 1936, it appeared with "Putting to Sea" and "M., Singing" under the title "Three Poems."[42] All deal with the subconscious nature of truth. "M., Singing" is in part 3 of *The Sleeping Fury* along with the title poem. The initial stands for "Maidie," the nickname of Bogan's daughter, Mathilde. In her daughter's singing, the poet hears the reverberations of dreams. Imagery again suggests "Medusa" in the "long harvest which they reap/In the sunk land of dust and flame" ("The grass will always be growing for hay/Deep on the ground" and "the yellow dust" in "Medusa"). But in this later poem, the "beings" become less fearsome as they leave to "move to space beneath our sky." In poetry, as in music, Bogan finds recognition of truth in symbols, in the emotional abstractions of sounds and images.

Part 3 has only two other poems. One, "Rhyme," is a lyric in the Cavalier manner but with the mark of its twentieth-century writer in its fast-moving lines. It is the earlier influence, no doubt, that permits the " 'twas" of the third line in a time when Bogan was avoiding such language. Placed between "The Sleeping Fury" and "M., Singing," the poem affords a change of pace, but is not without its own anxious overtones.

> What laid, I said,
> My being waste?
> 'Twas your sweet flesh
> With its sweet taste,—
>
> Which, like a rose,
> Fed with a breath,

And at its full
Belied all death.

It's at springs we drink;
It's bread we eat,
And no fine body,
Head to feet,

Should force all bread
And drink together,
Nor be both sun
And hidden weather.

Ah no, it should not;
Let it be.
But once heart's feast
You were to me.
(81)

The section concludes with "Evening-Star," a poem about love that
is quite dissimilar to "Rhyme." Bogan wrote Roethke (when he was
worrying about sounding like Stanley Kunitz in a particular poem)
that it echoed Eliot's chorus about light in "The Rock."[43] However,
as Ruth Limmer points out in a footnote to the letter, Eliot's "O
Light Invisible, we praise Thee" is an entirely different poem, and
Bogan was seeking principally to comfort Roethke. Despite this, Bogan was aware of the influence of Eliot's poem on her own. The "Ave
Maria" is also an influence, which gives another layer of meaning to
the poem with the form bringing to mind the role of Mary as inter-
cessor for women in conjunction with the significance of the Roman
goddess for whom the planet Venus is named. There is also the irony
of using a suggestion of the Catholic form used to praise the Virgin
to invoke a pagan goddess of love. Along with the irony, there is a
certain melancholy in that neither love nor religion is wholly believed
or wholly relinquished.

"Putting to Sea"

Part 4 of *The Sleeping Fury* consists of six poems beginning with
"Spirit's Song" and ending with "Song for a Lyre" ("Putting to Sea"
and "Spirit's Song" are in reverse order in *Blue Estuaries*). Containing

the central poem "Putting to Sea" as well as shorter poems, it continues the exploration of the psychic changes maturity brings in both the expectations and fears of youth. As though not to begin with too solemn a note, "Spirit's Song" is a short, lightly rueful lyric. "Putting to Sea" immediately follows. Of this poem, Bogan said, "I know what it's about, with my upper reason, just a little; it came from pretty far down, thank God."[44] She had at an earlier stage of writing called it "Goodbye at Sea"—"which will sum up the Holden suffering, endured so long, but now, at last, completely over."[45] Because it comes from the subconscious, the meaning is enveloped in symbols but is less obscure than in some earlier poems. Unlike the symbolism described by the first voice in "Summer Wish"—"Malicious symbol, key for rusty wards, / The crafty knight in the game, with its mixed move, / Prey to an end not evident to craft"—the symbolism of a sea journey, of fertile and sterile nature, of the sea itself, in "Putting to Sea" is less a "mixed move." Human experience is paralleled in nature and the seasons. The fruitful summer of life is left behind, and only a false season of summer can be seen ahead; but before reaching that shore, there is respite in feeling the sea of life beneath. Even so, there is obscurity in the nature of the sterile land ahead. Why must the shores be sterile? And why is it that "there, out of metal, and to light obscene, / The flamy blooms burn backwards to their seed"? Given that the early period of fruition is behind, why is maturity to be barren? The answer seems to be in the next to last stanza: the heart is still bruised by hate.

Three versions in typescript and manuscript show that Bogan worked to eliminate such lines as "A dreadful dream has caught us in its bound," "Do we deserve no better, our remorse / So strong," and "Dismissed, rejected rides / This bark."[46] The poem develops toward the philosophy indicated in the line "Motion beneath us, fixity above," an expression of the universal pattern that is larger than life. The last stanza reiterates the philosophy of Rilke in the lines Bogan quoted to Roethke when he was emotionally ill and hospitalized:

> Bend to the chart, in the extinguished night
> Mariners! Make way slowly; stay from sleep;
> That we may have short respite from such light.
>
> And learn, with joy, the gulf, the vast, the deep.

She described in her letter her own experience in a hospital:

> Well, there I was, and I got worse and worse, rather than better and better, because I hadn't come into myself as a person, and was still a puling child, hanging on to people, and trying to make them tell me the truth. . . . You won't be THAT foolish. The good old normal world is really a lot of fun, once you give in to it, and stop fighting against it. Fight with your work, but let the world go on, bearing you and being borne by you: that's the trick. As old Rilke said:

> > *Und wenn dich das Irdische vergass,*
> > *zu der stillen Erde sag: Ich rinne.*
> > *Zu dem raschen Wasser sprich: Ich bin.*[47]

(In a footnote, the editor of the letters identifies the lines as being from sonnet 29 of *The Sonnets to Orpheus,* part 2, and translates them as: "And if the worldly forget you, say to the silent earth: I flow. To the swift water say: I am.")

Appearance and Reality

The need to give up old and harmful ways of feeling is the subject of "Kept," the poem following "Putting to Sea." Like the dolls in Yeats's poem in *Responsibilities* who considered a human baby "a noisy and filthy thing," the dolls and other toys of "Kept" are the childish feelings that deny the adult nature. Bogan's poem is similar in rhythm and form to Yeats's "The Dolls," as well, and may have been influenced by his poem since, as she said, she had been influenced when young by *Responsibilities*. In his notes, Yeats explains the impetus for his poem: "I had noticed once again how all thought among us is frozen into 'something other than human life.' "[48] In Bogan's poem the toys "get broken in the play," the childish ways are outgrown; but in Yeats's there is no change.

Bogan often refers in her poems to a "mask" that stands between the true personality and the world, or between knowledge and ignorance. Yeats, of course, used the symbol, as Bogan was aware (she wrote in a review: "In 1909 Yeats begins to speak of 'the mask,' and to write those direct poems filled with scorn for 'Paudeen' and Paudeen's wealthy 'betters.' *Responsibilities* [1914] developed this phrase fully").[49] In a poem of Yeats's called "The Mask," the barrier between lovers is unimportant "so there is but fire / In you, in me." The mask

is of a different nature in Bogan's "Heard by a Girl," although it too
arises between lovers. Here, it is not an attractive outer cover that
engages the other, but a "secret and . . . delicate mask" that protects
the self-concept. Rather than a dialogue as is Yeats's poem, whose
truth the reader must judge, the poem is a monologue presented with
an adult awareness of youthful naivete and error that makes the tone
ironic:

> Something said: You have nothing to fear
> From those long fine bones, and that beautiful ear.
>
> From the mouth, and the eyes set well apart,
> There's nothing can come which will break your heart.
>
> From the simple voice, the indulgent mind,
> No venom breeds to defeat your kind.
>
> And even, it said, those hands are thin
> And large, well designed to clasp within
>
> Their fingers (and O what more do you ask?)
> The secret and the delicate mask.
>
> (88)

The poem that follows, "Packet of Letters," in which old letters pre-
serve a painful time, is a more directly bitter look at a failed love.[50]
The letters in a drawer "rave and grieve" and give off coldness. The
poem concludes "There, there, the thugs of the heart did murder. /
There, still in murderers' guise, two stand embraced, embalmed."

A Working Through

The Sleeping Fury closes on a peaceful note, indicating a working
through of conflicting feelings. Bogan wrote "Song for a Lyre" after
visiting Edmund Wilson at Trees, a house in Stamford, Connecticut.
As she wrote him later (the "Russian steppe" reference is perhaps to
work being done by Wilson at the time leading to *To the Finland
Station*):

Dear Edmund:
Haunted by your woods, I came home and produced a love poem to end
love poems—perhaps the only real love poem I ever wrote—and I plan to

have it stand against winter and silence and hatred and party politics (if need be, in italics) at the end of my book. (The Sleeping Furry, a Tale of the Russian Steppes, by L. B., dedicated to E.W., in hatitude.)[51]

The peaceful tone of "Song for a Lyre" did not evolve without struggle. She wrote John Wheelock: "All my black side tried to stop it from coming, but it would come, and it came just the way it is: all of a piece."[52]

> The landscape where I lie
> Again from boughs sets free
> Summer; all night must fly
> In wind's obscurity
> The thick, green leaves that made
> Heavy the August shade.
>
> Soon, in the pictured night,
> Returns—as in a dream
> Left after sleep's delight—
> The shallow autumn stream:
> Softly awake, its sound
> Poured on the chilly ground.
>
> Soon fly the leaves in throngs;
> O love, though once I lay
> Far from its sound, to weep,
> When night divides my sleep,
> When stars, the autumn stream,
> Stillness, divide my dream,
> Night to your voice belongs.
>
> (90)

What Bogan called her "black side" continued to interfere with her impulse to write, despite her progress toward serenity. "I don't think I will write very much more," she wrote in October 1938.[53] She did, however, but so infrequently that *The Sleeping Fury* was to be her last book of new poems.

Chapter Eight
Poems and New Poems

Literary Fashion

Poetry was necessary to Bogan, both the work of other poets and her own; but poetry as she felt it to be was not in fashion, and this discouraged her. She leaned upon the function of formal literary traditions because, as I have said, they answered a true need for her. When Bogan's mother died on December 26, 1936, the poet read Yeats for comfort and remembered Christopher Isherwood's "The Novaks" ("It helped me to bear my mother's death, thus functioning as some people believe art should").[1] She told Roethke, "[A]s far as I'm concerned, you can have anyone who writes 'odic poems.' I'm going right back to pure music."[2] A lyric should be either a song or an epigram, she believed.[3] This belief in the lyric as emotional analogue or emotion combined with wit served to lessen her productivity as periods of intense feeling or opinion grew fewer (but not less intense) with increasing age. In the process of commenting to Roethke on a poem of his, she said, "It really is much better to write about objects and people and things, unless a great convulsion takes place within, and tears you apart willy-nilly. These convulsions do not occur very often, as time goes on, I find, and when they do occur, they soon pass off."[4]

Bogan was disaffected with the literary cultural milieu of the time. She wrote May Sarton on April 24, 1940:

What can be done concerning the general distrust and even hatred shown toward lyric poetry, so prevalent now, I can't think. Nothing, I suppose. These turns of the wheel of taste always happen; the distrust of form and emotion is always present, in every generation. The particular form this distrust takes, in our day, may be symptomatic of a social neurosis that only the future can trace down and name.[5]

To John Wheelock, who proposed that she publish a collected edition of poems, she commented:

98

The American cultural situation is now lower than it has ever been before, so far as conscious art is concerned. . . . All this means that there will be a poetry "revival" in about fifty years: maybe twenty-five. But I am so out of the general line, now; and I really have been so battered about that I don't care any more.[6]

During 1937 she wrote three poems that reflect this state of mind. One, "Poem at Forty," expresses disappointed hope.[7] It was never published. Two others that were published that year also indicate a lack of faith in human fate. Besides disenchantment with the literary state, Bogan in these poems sees life as defeating. She chose not to collect them. "New Moon," published in August, contrasts the "Sweet curve, sweet light, new thin moon, now purely at ease" with the disasters that befall humanity beneath its light. It is the conflict of romantic aspiration and harsh reality ("purest along the edge of darkness infinite") that Bogan never really got over.[8] "Untitled" is a poem of the pain of disappointed romantic love in which lovers are seen as inevitably false.[9] These three poems, not very good poems, are of interest to indicate Bogan's state of mind at this time. She revealed her disapproval of them by neither collecting them nor publishing at all "Poem at Forty."

Epigrams and Light Verse

In the end, she agreed to her editor's suggestion to compile an edition of her poems. She added some new poems to those published in earlier volumes to compose *Poems and New Poems,* published in 1941. The new poems vary from epigrams to two important works, "The Dream" and "Come, Sleep . . . ," that belong to those poems of the subconscious that dominate her work. With parts 1 through 3 of the volume comprising the poems of *Body of This Death, Dark Summer,* and *The Sleeping Fury,* the new poems are in parts 4 and 5.

Part 4 consists of epigrams and light verse. But one poem, a rhymed book review written for Edmund Wilson, is a poem of substance. A brief look at the poems together is adequate to see their relationship to Bogan's other poems. The first, "Several Voices Out of a Cloud," is an acrimonious attack on the nature of literary fame:

> Come, drunks and drug-takers; come, perverts unnerved!
> Receive the laurel, given, though late, on merit; to whom
>   and wherever deserved.

Parochial punks, trimmers, nice people, joiners true-blue,
Get the hell out of the way of the laurel. It is deathless
     And it isn't for you.[10]

The epigrams, "Question in a Field" and "Solitary Observation
Brought Back from a Sojourn in Hell," are similar to the kind writ-
ten by Yeats. Like Yeats's "On Hearing That the Students of Our
New University Have Joined the Agitation Against Immoral Litera-
ture," the second one has a very long title for a very short poem.
Bogan's is shorter even than Yeats's:

          At midnight tears
          Run into your ears.
                    (98)

The undertone of grief in Bogan's satire makes it unsuccessful as an
epigram, I think, although one critic thought that "for an emotional
crisis, a minimum of words best expresses reality."[11]
     "Variation on a Sentence" is a droll extension of some words from
Thoreau's *Journals*, "There are few or no bluish animals":

          Of white and tawny, black as ink,
          Yellow, and undefined, and pink,
          And piebald, there are droves, I think.

          (Buff kine in herd, gray whales in pod,
          Brown woodchucks, colored like the sod,
          All creatures from the hand of God.)

          And many of a hellish hue;
          But, for some reason hard to view,
          Earth's bluish animals are few.
                    (99)

     Written with humor as a rhymed book review, "Animal, Vegeta-
ble and Mineral" is more than amusing. Under the guise of capital-
ized clichés, such as "Deepening Sense of Awe," there is real awe and
the driving Bogan need to understand. The book reviewed is *Glass
Flowers from the Ware Collection in the Botanical Museum of Hartford
University: Insect Pollination Series* by Fritz Kredel. Bogan has added
the epigraph from Jules Renard, "Dieu ne croit pas à notre Dieu"
(God does not believe in our God). The poem throughout expresses
wonder at the close interaction of design between bee and flower to

pollinate the flowers and give nectar to the bees, as in the ninth stanza:

> The dyer's greenwood waits the bee in tension.
> Petals are pressed down: then the stamens spring
> (The pistils, too) into a new dimension,
> Hitting the bee's back between wing and wing.
> Who thought this out? It passes comprehension.

In addition to this mystery, there is the wonder of the artists, father and son, who spent fifty years in making the glass flowers of the exhibit. The last line of the poem, set off by itself, is not at all satirical: "What Artist laughs? What clever Daemon thinks?"[12]

It is this metaphysical intellectual frame that prevents Bogan in other poems from being a successful writer of light verse. As anyone who reads her letters knows, Bogan was witty. She was very good at *bouts rimés,* too. But away from a social context, the impulse to write must have arisen from a complex of feelings that was too imbued with either unhappiness or the need to understand, or both, to be often truly light.

"Dream" Poems

Part 5 contains eleven poems, two of which are translations: "Kapuzinerberg (Salzburg)," from the French of Pierre-Jean Jouve, and "From Heine" *(Der Tod, das ist die kühle Nacht. . .).* Among the original poems, two concern the subconscious, specifically as it is revealed in dream.

"The Dream" is an actual nightmare she experienced, Bogan explained in a recorded discussion of the poem.[13] The horse, she said, is a symbol of overpowering force that one's moral force cannot cope with, and the other woman is a symbol of spiritual strength given in a crisis. When asked what the moral of the poem is, she replied that courage is better than cowardice. In other words, her mature nature understood and thereby overcame the childlike fear. Written in 1937 (Bogan observed her fortieth birthday in August of that year), the reference to "Fear kept for thirty-five years" is to her childhood. She wrote Sister Angela in 1966:

"The Dream" is a later poem, written in my late thirties, after a complete change in my way of living, and in my general point of view about life (and the universe at large!). It is the actual transcript of "a nightmare," but there

is reconciliation involved with the fright and horror. It is through the possibility of such reconciliations that we, I believe, manage to live.[14]

And in a letter to May Sarton, Bogan said:

"The Dream," by the way, is a poem of victory and of release. The terrible
power, which may v. well be the psychic demon, is tamed and placated, but
not destroyed; the halter and the bit were already there, and something was
done about *control* and *understanding*.[15]

As in "The Sleeping Fury," the destructive emotions are neutral-
ized when squarely faced. I think it indicative of Bogan's metaphysical bent, with her admixture of romanticism, to think in terms of a
"psychic demon" rather than a "logical" effect of emotional force.

Stanley Kunitz, in his review of *Poems and New Poems,* recognized
the importance of "The Dream" to Bogan's work and the submerged
nature of its meaning:

But I am persuaded that the true world of Miss Bogan's imagination, of
which she has up to now given us only fragmentary impressions, is "the
sunk land of dust and flame," where an unknown terror is king, presiding
over the fable of a life, in the deep night swarming with images of reproach
and desire. Out of that underworld she has emerged with her three greatest
poems, spaced years between, of which the latest is *The Dream. . . .* In the
body of Miss Bogan's work *The Dream* stands with *Medusa* and *The Sleeping
Fury* in violence of statement, in depth of evocation. They give off the taste
of pomegranates: Persephone might have written them.[16]

I believe that another such poem of "the fable of a life" is "Come,
Sleep . . . ," another "dream" poem that is a reflection on the nature
of dream rather than on an actual dream. The poem has been discussed in the first chapter; however, in the context of this chapter I
would like to point out the last two lines. The "dark turreted house"
that "reflects itself / In the depthless stream" recalls imagery from
Bogan's childhood. She mentions having been born in a turreted
house in a letter to John Wheelock ("I'll send them a picture of my
birthplace, which will strike them dumb, I am sure. The house has
such a cupola and eaves made of gingerbread").[17] In her poem, "The
Cupola," the room is the place of the mirror that brings "negligent
death" indoors. And "the depthless stream" echoes the psychological
deep of "Journey Around My Room." At the same time, the imagery

is available to all without losing meaning. As in "The Dream," psychological truth is a combination of image and the form of sound and rhythm.

"Zone," also discussed previously, is in this section. As I said, I find it didactic and not of the impact of "The Dream" and "Come, Sleep . . . . " "To an Artist, to Take Heart," the epigraph derived from a longer poem and with more substance than the two epigraphs in part 4, is placed after "The Dream," a context that suggests poetry as the reconciler of psychic tension.

The Impetus to Poetry

With Bogan's practice of changing pace from the serious, the next poem in the volume is the melodic lyric, "To Be Sung on the Water," taken from the title of a song by Schubert.[18] Beginning "Beautiful, my delight / Pass, as we pass the wave," it has a regularity of rhythm established by the three accented syllables in each line and an *ababa cdefddf* rhyme scheme, and a soothing repetition of *s* sounds that are suggestive of the peaceful movement of a boat through water. But there is also an observation of the transitoriness of experience in the idea of delight as being as self-limiting as are the passing wave and the light and shadow of night—with the suggestion of the stream as metaphor for the ongoing life force in which the boaters dip their oar. Delight becomes "Less than the sound of its blade / Dipping the stream once more." In "Musician," which follows, music is used, it seems to me, as a symbol of the fruition of will and wisdom. That the fruition is achieved by a certain giving up of strong or personal feeling is indicated by the adjectives "thin," "lonely," and "cool" in the first two stanzas and in the words "slow" and "the long / String it was born to know" in the third. This philosophy of distance, of the overriding nature of the pattern larger than the individual, is made explicit in "Cartography" in which the "chart / Of artery and vein" on the hand is seen as parallel to other life patterns:

> Mapped like the great
> Rivers that rise
> Beyond our fate
> And distant from our eyes.

The section is completed with a parody of Auden, "Evening in the
Sanitarium," and the final lyric, "The Daemon." One of a group of
parodies published in the *Nation* in 1938 under the title "Five Parodies," "Evening in the Sanitarium" carried "(Imitated from Auden)"
under the title.[19] The poem is in theme and tone very close to Bogan's own work, despite its parody of what John Malcolm Brinnin
calls Auden's "tendency, particularly in his early poems, to make so-
ciological observations in clinical terms and to view the world as an
enormous hospital in which everyone is a patient."[20] As in "The Long
Walk," the patients are described from Bogan's firsthand experience,
or at least her imagination inspired by firsthand experience, in sani-
tariums. The tone of "You will be again as normal and selfish and
heartless as anybody else" reflects Bogan's own feeling, and the overall emotional emptiness and lack of hope mirrors the mental state of
illness.[21]

But Bogan did not let the volume end on this dispirited note. The
last poem indicates her surviving need to write. Of "The Daemon"
she wrote May Sarton in 1959:

It is wonderful to know that my poems *spoke* to you: "The Daemon" especially, which was written (given!) one afternoon almost between one curb
of a street and another. *Why not?* is always a great help. God presses us so
hard, often, that we rebel—and we should. Auden once told me that we
should *talk back* to God; that this is a kind of prayer.[22]

The Daemon

Must I tell again
In the words I know
For the ears of men
The flesh, the blow?

Must I show outright
The bruise in the side,
The halt in the night,
And how death cried?

Must I speak to the lot
Who little bore?
It said *Why not?*
It said *Once more.*

T. S. Eliot, later, in his "Three Voices of Poetry," also conceived of the poetic impulse as a demon. He said of the poet that "he is haunted by a demon, a demon against which he feels powerless, because in its first manifestation it has no face, no name, nothing; and the words, the poem he makes, are a kind of form of exorcism of this demon."[23] Bogan continued to write when under this kind of impetus, but the impetus came infrequently. In the over thirty years remaining to her, she wrote only fifteen or so poems that she still liked when she selected poems for her final collection.

Chapter Nine
Collected Poems, 1923–1953

A Looking-back

When the next collected volume appeared in 1953, there were few poems that were not in the older collection. The only new poems in *Collected Poems 1923–1953* are "After the Persian I, II, III, IV, V," "Train Tune," and "Song for the Last Act." All are a looking-back over life, a view of life from the end. Because Bogan was middle-aged, not old, at the time she wrote these poems, it seems strange that this vantage point should be exclusive. Perhaps the first realization of the end of life that comes with middle age had the strongest impact.

The years between the publication of *Poems and New Poems* in 1941 and *Collected Poems* in 1953 were busy ones for Bogan. She reviewed for the *New Yorker* and other magazines, served on prize committees (including that which awarded the first Bollingen Prize to Ezra Pound in 1948), was a visiting instructor at the University of Washington (summer 1948), the University of Chicago (1949), and the University of Arkansas (1952), and served as Consultant in Poetry at the Library of Congress, 1945–46. She compiled for the Library of Congress *Works in the Humanities Published in Great Britain, 1939–1946* (published in 1950), wrote *Achievement in American Poetry, 1900–1950* (1951), and, with Elizabeth Meyer, translated Goethe's *Werther* in 1948. She also talked of writing a "long prose thing" to be based on her memories but seems never to have written very much of it. In 1948 she wrote Katharine S. White, fiction and poetry editor of the *New Yorker*:

So now I go to bed at night, and lie awake in the morning, turning over the "stories" in my refreshed mind. They will be memories, and, since I am not the "confessing" type, it is hard to start them off. I tend to surround the facts with a certain amount of "philosophy," as well; and that is not good. I intend to throw the material onto paper v. soon, however; and then shape it afterward. Criticism, when practiced over years, makes the creative side rather timid.[1]

She wrote very little poetry, either. Perhaps an uncollected poem printed in *Voices* in 1951 tells something about the nature of this hiatus in saying that "words do not come to the old prayer":

The Catalpa Tree

Words do not come to the old prayer,—only the rung names
    and the pauses.
An autumn I remember only by the pods of the catalpa tree
    that did not fall.
Tears were shed, sobbed to wild herbs in a field, whatever their
    causes,
And a house had a wall like a web of thorns about it. I
    remember that wall.

Only the long pods remained; the tree was drained like a sieve.
Perhaps the secret voice you hear under your mouth was all I
    could keep:
The burnished pods not claimed by a wizened month once said
    I should live.
They hang in my song of another autumn, in this hour stolen
    from sleep.[2]

She seems to be going back over disturbing childhood memories that are more "directly" voiced in poetry than in prose. Poetry can express "the hour stolen from sleep," the subconscious, that prose shies away from; yet the threatening nature of these buried feelings destroys serenity. She touched upon this dilemma in a remark to Morton Zabel in 1952 (in the context of praising some old letters of his she had come upon) : "This is the line we should re-discover, and fruitfully explore, in our 50's and 60's. No moaning over the dark mysteries, but a continued thorough exploration of what mysterious Life and equally mysterious Self have to offer."[3] The trouble was that mysterious Life and mysterious Self were bound up with the dark mysteries.

"After the Persian"

"After the Persian," first published (part 1) in the *New Yorker* in 1951 and in *Poetry* (parts 1–4) in 1952, before the addition of Part 5

and inclusion in *Collected Poems,* makes clear that Bogan fears these
"dark mysteries": "I do not wish to know / The depths of your terrible jungle. . . . I am the dweller on the temperate threshold." It
is a settling for peace, but a reaching beyond only that in the metaphysical predisposition: "And the day stains with what seems to be
more than the sun / What may be more than my flesh." There are
many of the elements of "A Tale," written when Bogan was very
young, in "After the Persian."[4] Like the earlier poem, it has an exotic
locale and treats life as a quest with the difference that the quest is
over. The "light" is found, but the "something dreadful and another"
of "A Tale" is avoided rather than conquered; it is "in the lowest
layer of the dream." The lines of "After the Persian," moving more
slowly, have a calmer tone. Bogan explained to May Sarton what she
meant by "eight-sided, like my heart" in the last line of part 2: "The
octagonal here is somehow symbolic of freedom. Love of things, I
suppose, understood, more than love of human beings. . . . The delight in objects, both natural and artifacts, which has grown in me
ever since the *obsessive* person was left behind (or buried, if you like,
in the lowest layer of the dream)."[5] It is a kind of resignation from
love rather than a real reconciliation with the limitations of humanity. Part 2 contains the lines:

> The hunt sweeps out upon the plain
> And the garden darkens.
> They will bring the trophies home
> To bleed and perish

The trophies bleed and perish, but a heart can be trained not to care
if the world does not understand their worth.

The first line of part 3, "All has been translated into treasure,"
indicates that life has been experienced and assimilated, and the poetry has been written. It is a strange theme for a poem with such
evidence of joy in creativity. The romantic exoticism of the almost-
parallel construction, the musical rhythm, and the vivid imagery be-
lie the statement of depletion. Instead they indicate that aspiration is
frustrated rather than dead. Part 5 confirms the situation:

> Goodbye, goodbye!
> There was so much to love, I could not love it all;
> I could not love it enough.

Some things I overlooked, and some I could not find.
Let the crystal clasp them
When you drink your wine, in autumn.[6]

"Train Tune" is placed between "After the Persian" and "Song for
the Last Act" as a light poem. It has the quick rhythm and fast-moving images of scenes seen from a moving train as the lines go back
over life to conclude: "Back along love/Back through midnight."

"Song for the Last Act"

"Song for the Last Act" is both lyrically musical, as the title word
"song" indicates, and deeply reflective. Like "Fifteenth Farewell" it
combines beauty of form and image with a serious, personal meaning.
Also, like "Fifteenth Farewell," it has a semiserious title, as though
unconsciously apologizing for the personal meaning. The first stanza,
using the imagery of summer moving into fall and beginning "Now
that I have your face by heart, I look/Less at its features than its
darkening frame," contains imagery of statuary in a garden immune
to passing seasons, reminiscent of the statue of the girl in the earlier
poem "Statue and Birds" in its contrast between life and inert matter.
Unlike the statue in the earlier poem, however, who seems to yearn
for life, the "lead and marble figures" of "Song for the Last Act"
watch "in insolent ease" the seasonal change. The tone of the poem
is one of mature assessment, "a voyage done." There is no youthful
aspiration here.[7]

The second stanza, beginning "Now that I have your voice by
heart," evidences the creative difficulty ("The staves are shuttled over
with a stark unprinted silence") in a context of imagery of the subconscious ("In a double dream/I must spell out the storm, the running stream"). Although mutability can be seen in the context of
universal time and emotions in the context of the human lot, there
is no reconciliation in having the "voice by heart," merely acknowledgment of its overwhelming nature. In the six-page manuscript of
work on the poem, this stanza has several significant changes.[8] One
version beginning "Now that I have your head by heart" contains the
lines: "The text as baffling as a book in a dream/The meaning shuttled over with the stark/Symbolic utterance I cannot heed." Then another version beginning "Now that I have your heart by heart" that
is a reworking of the one above it. Then one beginning "Now that I

have your words by heart." Finally, the change to "Now that I have
your voice by heart," as well as the gradual change of the other lines.
About five versions in all of the stanza whose meaning remains essentially the same, that what the poet has to say arises from a source she
cannot understand because it appears only in symbols, "prey to an
end not evident to craft."[9]

It is one of the best of Bogan's poems in its use of sound, imagery,
and form both to recreate the feeling of a psychological state and to
reflect upon it. Though Bogan was writing few poems, "After the
Persian" and "Song for the Last Act" were proof of undiminished poetic powers.

Chapter Ten
The Blue Estuaries

"Night"

In 1968 Bogan's last book of poems was published. *The Blue Estuaries,* the title she chose for her lifetime collection, derives from the second line of "Night," a poem obviously important in its expression of Bogan's poetic viewpoint. The word *night* occurs nowhere in the body of the poem, but by the line "In your narrowing dark hours" in the last stanza, it is clear that death is meant, death of the individual, of the poet. Though the individual dies, the causes and forces that influence life remain in operation. Whatever this larger plan, this universal area, is, it is cold and remote to the poet because it is both beyond life and beyond ken. Blue estuaries, like blood in a vein, carry the vital substance that advances the mysterious design and are operated by the same laws. Vital substance is what her poems were to Bogan and to her reach to understand the larger meaning.

In the imagery of the islands, winds, tides, and patterned stars, with "the pulse clinging to the rocks," there is the feeling of eternal movement and the inconsequentiality of the particular and temporal. There is the sense of what is meant by Rilke's words: "How small is that with which we struggle; / How great is that which struggles with us":

> The cold remote islands
> And the blue estuaries
> Where what breathes, breathes
> The restless wind of the inlets,
> And what drinks, drinks
> The incoming tide;
>
> Where shell and weed
> Wait upon the salt wash of the sea,
> And the clear nights of stars
> Swing their lights westward
> To set behind the land;

Where the pulse clinging to the rocks
Renews itself forever;
Where, again on cloudless nights,
The water reflects
The firmament's partial setting;

—O remember
In your narrowing dark hours
That more things move
Than blood in the heart.

(130)

"Night" was first published with its companion piece, "Morning," in
Poetry in 1962.[1] "Morning" emphasizes living rather than dying—the
aspect of the grand design that preserves the species. The poem is
divided into two numbered, five-line stanzas, each of which comments upon a phenomenon of natural survival. In the first, the poet
observes that the green-blue eggs of the robins are the complementary
color to the birds' rosy breasts and then asks, "Is it a vision in the
eyes, a resolution in the blood/That calls back these birds, to cherish
and to guard?" Implications touching upon the role of beauty in survival are here, joined in consideration with the more generally ac-
knowledged instincts of the blood. Why do the robins "cherish" and
"guard"?

The second stanza describes a tendril of convolvulus, a vine, which
winds around a rose branch "avoiding/All but the smaller thorns."
The adjectives of the first line, "clever and as though instructed,"
make it clear that the living pattern of the vine is being regarded by
the poet in terms of human living patterns. In the third line, "Having chosen the rosebranch for the support of its ascending spiral," the
word "chosen" has human implications, especially perhaps in conjunction with a thorny "ascending" path. The nature of the life drive
seems to be the question, as well as how much of human life and art
is bound up in this drive.

In these last poems, Bogan is concerned primarily with the metaphysical questions of essence and meaning, both as they apply to the
larger whole and as they apply to the individual. The difference between reality and human aspiration is as baffling from the last of life
as it was from the beginning. The mind which strives to order is still
victim of destructive emotional forces arising from early, uncompre-

hended events, so that the individual essence is almost as unknowable as the universal.

Last Years

In these last years, Bogan found herself again oppressed by old psychic wounds. She went through another seige of depression, another hospitalization, and, though better, she was still struggling until her death in February 1970. In a letter dated June 1965 she wrote from the Neurological Institute: "This depressed state began last fall, I think—with the return to the scenes of my childhood—or adolescence. Boston is really filled with sorrowful memories of my family, and my early self.—I thought, because I had 'insight' into it all, that I could rise above it. But [Dr.] H. has told me that a depression can *seep through,* as it were, in any case."[2] *The Blue Estuaries* is dedicated "To the memory of my father, mother and brother."

Of the twelve poems in the new volume not previously collected, four had been written, at least in some form, in an earlier period, leaving only eight to be written in the fifteen years between *Collected Poems* and *The Blue Estuaries.* There is evidence in manuscripts that Bogan worked on other poems. She continued to be busy writing reviews and articles, teaching from time to time, working on prize committees, and translating (with Elizabeth Mayer) *The Glass Bees* by Ernst Juenger (1961), *Elective Affinities* by Goethe (1963), and *The Sorrows of Young Werther* and *Novella* by Goethe (1971), and (with Elizabeth Roget) *The Journal of Jules Renard* (1964).[3] Two collections of her criticism, *Selected Criticism* (1955) and *A Poet's Alphabet* (1970), were published, as well as (with William Jay Smith) an anthology of poems for young people, *The Golden Journey* (1965).

Objective Poems

Section 6, containing the newly collected poems in *The Blue Estuaries,* begins with "The Dragonfly," written in 1961.[4] It was interpreted in engraved glass for Steuben Glass by George Thompson and Bruce Moore.[5] Of "The Dragonfly" Bogan wrote, "It is all based on FACT. And I am rather proud of the last line—which is a piece of pure 'inspiration.' Get those repeated *u* sounds—one of them disguised"[6] (this line reads "With the other husks of summer"). Despite her claim that the poem is based on fact, the meaning is a metaphys-

ical one of "design and purpose." Every statement of fact is framed in
a context of wonder at that fact. The dragonfly is, in "fact," metaphor for the larger life force which drives and consumes the individual. Bogan was aware of this, undoubtedly, and intended her
statement to mean that the data, as in "Animal, Vegetable and Mineral," are illustrative of a truth beyond knowledge.

An earlier poem, "St. Christopher," written about 1940 and re-
written in 1956, published in *Art News* ("Poets on Painting") in
1958, is a reaction to a fifteenth-century copy of a fresco which is in
the Metropolitan Museum.[7] In the look of devotion on the face of
Christopher for the Christ Child, Bogan sees the hope of the world
and contrasts the intensity of the saint with the manners and mimicry
of the middle class. His authenticity is his strength which brings the
Child to safety. To Bogan the need for the artist to be authentic, to
avoid the mere absorption of the thoughts and feelings of polite society, was a strongly held conviction. In a lecture, "Popular and Un-
popular Poetry in America," delivered in 1944 at the University of
Michigan for the Hopwood series, she admonished young writers to
"stand outside middle-class art."[8]

Another poem written in 1940 and published later is "The Sorcerer's Daughter," which, along with "The Young Mage" (written in
1957), was in a special number, "The American Imagination," of the
Times Literary Supplement in 1959.[9] The poem is an ironic comment
on fate as well as upon the conventional signs of auspicious romance
in which everything can seem promisingly right one moment only to
come to naught the next. In an entirely different tone, "The Young
Mage" re-creates the magic expectation of youth that has implicit in
its energy eventual destruction as well. It has short, incantatory lines
like an old nursery rhyme and intense imagery, but ends:

> . . . Beware
> Of the round web swinging from the angle
> Of the steep stair,
> And of the comet's hair.

Written at the same time as "The Sorcerer's Daughter" and re-
written in 1956,[10] "March Twilight" voices a reaction to an affecting
quality of light. In mentioning the poem to John Wheelock, Bogan
said, "You and I both (and Léonie [Adams], too) have a thing about
equinoctial light!"[11] Both the metaphysical concern with meaning

and romantic aspiration are evident in this poem which begins, "This light is loss backward" and ends, "A watcher in these new, late beams might well see another face/And look into Time's eye, as into a strange house, for what lies within."

As though a companion poem, "July Dawn" follows in the volume. Rewritten in 1956 from a year-old draft, it was published separately in folio in 1957.[12] Its comment upon aspiration is ironic: "In that short moment/That makes all symbols lucky/Before we read them rightly." Even so, as the waning moon disappears, it is moving toward the time of waxing:

> Down to the dark it swam,
> Down to the dark it moved,
> Swift to that cluster of evenings
> When curved toward the full it sharpens.
>   (128)

"The Meeting"

One of those central poems that deal with the subconscious comes next, "The Meeting." Bogan's own remarks of explanation cannot be improved upon. The manuscript is dated "3 May 56,"[13] and on February 16, 1957, she wrote John Wheelock:

Your letter concerning "The Meeting" made me v. happy. The *materials* of that poem have haunted me for a long time; and I thought I must do it in prose. But one morning last spring the first lines hit me, and I sat on the corner of the chair and put them down. The rest came quite easily. I am glad you felt it to be "authentic." It certainly is the record of a recurring subconscious experience, concerning which I used to suffer a good deal; but now I am only curious and puzzled.[14]

She wrote Glenway Wescott on March 15: "It came out practically whole, although a few shifts had to be made. The change in the dream-creature's personality had taken place; the creature started out by being Raymond at his most guileful, of course. And I always thought of the locale at the *bottom* of the dream." And a year later (April 1958), she added in another letter to Wescott: "Now the encounter has faded out, a little.—I wait and wait to meet my *personus,* and the Wise Old Man, and other Jungian archetypes; but to little purpose. For one thing, I can't *stand* Wise Old Men."[15]

Whoever the personae of the dream are, the poem evokes both the

aura of dream and the conscious process of searching for the significance of the dream. The ephemeral and changing quality of dream is
in the dream-creature "whose smile dissolved" and in his second
smile toward a place beyond the dreamer, "no world of men." That
the dream is described in a frame of questioning ("Why do our paths
cross?") accents the irrational nature of the dream.

The Hold of the Subconscious

The mysterious area of the subconscious, and unconscious, and its
hold upon the conscious are also the subject of the concluding poems
of the volume. They are called "Three Songs" (and were printed as
such in the *New Yorker* in 1967).[16] Like music, they arise from structures or rhythms of the psyche. Bogan instructed Howard Moss of the
New Yorker: "These three 'songs' seem to go together, in this order—
although the third one is older than the other two. But it seems to
belong to the same world (of dream and aberration). The first and
second songs are new: this winter."[17]

The first and second songs are "Little Lobelia's Song" and "Psychiatrist's Song," both arising from Bogan's depression. "Little Lobelia's
Song" has been discussed in the first chapter, but it is relevant here
to add an illuminating remark made by Bogan in 1966 to Rufina
McCarthy Helmer (an old friend, a teacher of high school English):
"My strange little (for it *must* be a child-ghost, embedded in the subconscious) morning visitant is, I believe, yielding to work-exorcism,
more than to medication. *It* vanished at 10:30 A.M. today, and
hasn't been back. Work at the typewriter seems to bore it. For all it
wants to do is *weep*. O heavens, am I seeing the end of the tunnel, *at
last?*"[18]

Another voice from the poet's subconscious is projected onto the
voice of the psychiatrist in "Psychiatrist's Song." The manuscript has
"Song" crossed out of the title and "Recitative & Aria" substituted.[19]
In the recitative (the first thirteen lines), the psychiatrist reflects upon
his patient's early, harmful experiences and then, as though wearying
of human ills, in the aria moves away in his mind to a healing place
for both himself and his patient (the manuscript has a crossed-out line
that reads "As I would heal and receive"). I believe that the journey
is through the poet's subconscious as she imagines it reflected in the
psychiatrist's mind. For the dream-like land, reached by a boat, be-
longs to Bogan's symbolism (in "Zone," "Putting to Sea," and
"Night") as does, in the first stanza, the imagery from childhood of

"Those people, and that house, and that evening, seen/Newly above the dividing window sash—." The old family anxieties, the unknown regions of the subconscious and of death are haunting phantoms that must be bidden farewell in order to live on earth. The last lines, like a prayer, concede the difficulty:

> Farewell, phantoms of flesh and of ocean!
> Vision of earth
> Heal and receive me.

The third song is quite different. "Masked Woman's Song," "written circa 1940?" the manuscript says, was termed "a fairly old erotic song" by Bogan and concludes the volume as well as the "songs":[20]

> Before I saw the tall man
> Few women should see,
> Beautiful and imposing
> Was marble to me.
>
> And virtue had its place
> And evil its alarms,
> But not for that worn face,
> And not in those roped arms.
>   (136)

Perhaps the erotic seemed the unconscious force that was most closely tied to the universal; and, in that respect, this is the least personal of the three songs, an attempt to end on a note away from the painfully individual.

Some Final Remarks

The poems of *The Blue Estuaries* reflect an intelligent, serious, and extremely sensitive investigation of the meaning of life both for Bogan herself and for humanity in general—as she, characteristically deprecatingly, put it, "Bogan in cothurnus and Bogan in flat heels." The craftsmanship and artistry of the writing appeal through the rhythm and music and concentrated meaning of the words, through the use of line and stanza form, to both irrational and rational understanding. Poetry form serves to give shape to the otherwise chaotic or amorphous by bringing the emotional response of sound and rhythm as well as the intellectual response of acquired culture to the task. In Bogan's poems form always serves the meaning. It is never the other way around.

Symbol and metaphor are part of this form and part of psychological structure as well. This genuine use of form expresses in Bogan's poetry her revolt against the empty forms of society and of her own fears that would constrain her. Bogan looked into the subconscious, or unconscious, for personal meaning. The areas of dream and of fixed childhood images, of strong emotional impressions not rationally comprehended, are often the driving force behind a poem. She believed, as she said, that the unconscious knows more about us than we know about it and trusted the structures of symbols, rhythm, and line to express implicitly what could not be expressed explicitly. When a poem "came from pretty deep down" she considered it "a good sign." A lyric poem is "exigent," she said, and writing poetry was more satisfying to her than writing prose because poetry said what was to be said in a way that could be said in no other. Such distilled but often complex meaning can seem obscure at times because it deals with areas of the human mind that are not fully understood.

Both the primal, psychological impulses of all humanity—nature operating through the unconscious—and the buried psychological reactions to experience, the subconscious, motivate the poems. When experience is the motivating impulse, however, it is not a narrowly personal experience, nor indeed the experience itself, but rather the deeply felt reaction to experience that is the subject of the poem, a reaction that is part of all human sensation.

Bogan's personal images are those of such poems as "Medusa," "Old Countryside," "Summer Wish," "The Sleeping Fury," "The Dream," "Come, Sleep . . .," "Song for the Last Act," "The Meeting," "Psychiatrist's Song," and "Little Lobelia's Song" in which childhood fears, or adult anxieties about betrayal that result from childhood fears, are invoked. Images of a significant house, of a window, of mirrors, of a shell in which the sea can be heard, of the millstream, and of a force that threatens to overpower are examples that recur and are linked to her early life. But even without knowing the details of that life, the reader of the poems responds to the elemental fears of rejection, harm, or death. The personal experience is distilled by symbol and the emotional response to sound into common human experience.

In her rejection of what she considered the too subjective, Bogan turned to nature for objectivity. That the title of Bogan's final collection, *The Blue Estuaries,* is a reference to nature indicates the importance of the natural world in forming Bogan's mature philosophy. Anthropologist Gregory Bateson in his book *Mind and Nature: A Necessary Unity* declares: "What is *my* answer to the question of the nature of knowing? I surrender to the belief that my knowing is a small part of a wider integrated knowing that knits the entire biosphere or creation."[21] I find a similar belief implicit in the role of nature in Bogan's poetry. The late poem, "Night," in particular, is another way of stating the same view. But from her earliest poetry, Bogan assumes a universal pattern of existence of which nature and humanity are a part—a pattern that envelops both and far outreaches in significance the particulars of either. While the human is seen as above the rest of nature, it is subject to the same overriding forces and designs. In her letter to May Sarton in 1954, quoted in chapter 5, in which she tried to explain what she saw as the human relationship to nature in general, her words indicate that although "the same current runs through the whole set-up—natural and human," there is a division—perhaps that of the religious view of the divine spark in man (a residue of her religious experience)—between humanity and the rest of nature. However, her poems suggest a closer affinity of the human and the natural world than these words would indicate. In "Baroque Comment," for instance, the first stanza considers the violence and chance of creation as "coincident with" the vices of mankind although humanity triumphs in the last stanza with order, knowledge, wisdom, nobility, love—but above all, art. Art is the essence of human nature, a necessary ordering of the human experience that includes the "significant blood and the tears" mentioned in the same letter.

Life is seen as cyclic and patterned, intertwined with the cycles and patterns of the universe. The seasons of the year and the blossoms and ripening fruit and grain they bring are recurring metaphors for the stages of life, as are stones, water, and the tides for the prevailing quality of earth. But humanity is aware that life is a process to death and resists mutability at the same time that it is intensely involved in living. This is the dilemma that has often obsessed poets, of course, and many of Bogan's poems seek to understand the inherent tragedy. In this seeking, she finds consolation in the ongoing universe which is removed from pain.

Although Bogan's poems often mourn the sacrifice of the individual life to universal life, her later poems increasingly move beyond
the importance of the single to the larger whole. It is this tension
between the temporary and the timeless that operates in Bogan's concern with nature. It is the division made by time between the particular and the whole. As her poem "Division" says: "Though assailed
and undone is the green/Upon the wall and the sky:/Time and the
tree stand there." But though "time and the tree" remain, it is the
human lot to question the meaning of the drives and intricate forms
of life—the transformation in the human of the power which runs
through all that Bogan spoke about in her letter to May Sarton. An
example of this investigation is "Come, Sleep . . ." with its questioning of the "forms and appetites" of natural existence that seem to
be without the troubled consciousness of humanity.

In her poems Bogan seems to "read" nature for its human implications, for a glimpse of the "that which struggles with us" of Rilke's
statement. She marvels in "The Dragonfly" at the force and design of
an insect that goes through metamorphosis only to "fall/With the
other husks of summer." The winter swan with his "eyes in hiding"
is asked the rhetorical question, "Where lies the leaf-caught world
once thought abiding?" The knowledge sought gives qualified comfort, for although there may be philosophical peace in the larger
view, the individual struggle remains. "Summer Wish" looks most
closely at the patterns of nature for corresponding human patterns
and finds some hope in them; but "Night" sees the universal design
as a cold, remote, impersonal, ongoing force that provides the theater
for the crucially particular. Even though the knowledge "That more
things move/Than blood in the heart" gives only a qualified comfort,
however, there is still affirmation in the nature of the human mind
and heart which comprehends the immensity of life beyond the im-
mediate self and time.

Chapter Eleven
Bogan and the Critics

Louise Bogan began writing in the early part of the century when modern psychology and psychiatry were just entering the culture, and people at large were not used to examining the subconscious for meaning. After Freud and his followers became better known, there were still misconceptions about the feminine psyche. Critics who reviewed her poetry, with few exceptions, classed her with other "women poets" ("poetesses") and started from their preconceived idea of what women's poetry is, although in the case of Bogan, they tended to be surprised that, as Theodore Roethke said, "Louise Bogan is something else."[1] Neither in men nor in women was there the cultural insight into the workings of human nature that would predispose an understanding of her poems.

Nevertheless, her poems were liked and honored by some of the most discerning literary people, writers and critics, of her time. That her poetry should be appreciated in spite of its perceived obscurity is, I believe, because her form is so true to psychological structures that readers react emotionally even when they do not understand intellectually. Elder Olson remarked that her poems are felt but not understood: "her poems are like pictures of scenes from some passionate and bitter play which we have not seen."[2] Ford Madox Ford, in his review of *The Sleeping Fury,* said that when he read the first words of "Henceforth, from the Mind," he had this reaction:

You might almost think that the real poet, whether he write in prose or verse, taking up his pen, causes with the scratching on the paper such a vibration that that same vibration continues through the stages of being typed, set up in print, printed in magazine, and then in a book—that that same vibration continues right through the series of processes till it communicates itself at last to the reader and makes him say as I said when I read those words of Miss Bogan's: "This is authentic."[3]

Eda Lou Walton, in the *Nation,* said of the same volume, "One is impressed by a kind of wisdom in these poems, the wisdom of profound intuition and of a rapier analysis turned inward rather than outward."[4] Later, reviewing *Collected Poems,* John Ciardi said that Bogan sees the jungle within not only herself but everyone.[5] Richard Eberhart agreed in his review of *Collected Poems:* "A profundity of psychological knowledge works in the poems. One feels that truths of life, death and love have been confronted and uncompromising answers given."[6]

Hayden Carruth spoke of her technique as though it were separate from the power of what he called a "private inner violence." He termed the technique a "mask one must wear" without realizing the structural nature of the mask. He saw the first stanza of "Roman Fountain" as "a miraculous example of the power to bend the reader's actual bodily attitude, through phrasing, meter, and rhyme, to the movement of the poet's own vision" without seeing that he was describing more than craft. He knew there was more, even if he did not see it there, and went on to add: "But other readers [than those 'who take joy in prosodic effects for their own sake'] will seek for something more, the intact poetic experience, and they will go more often to simpler poems, 'Women,' 'Henceforth, from the Mind,' 'Short Summary,' 'To My Brother,' 'Man Alone,' 'Song for the Last Act,' and others. These are the poems in which the balance is exactly struck."[7]

Theodore Roethke was more aware than most of the manner in which the formal elements of Bogan's poetry function. He spoke of "the great variety and surety of her rhythms—that clue to the energy of the psyche" and said further that "Louise Bogan rarely, if ever, repeats a cadence, and this in an age when some poets achieve a considerable reputation with two or three or even *one* rhythm. The reason for this is, I believe, her absolute loyalty to the particular emotion." Roethke also commented that Bogan "never writes a serious poem until there is a genuine 'upwelling' from the unconscious; who shapes emotion into an inevitable-seeming, an endurable, form."[8]

Morton Zabel spoke of the "poetic truth" of Bogan's poetry. In a long review of *The Sleeping Fury,* he pointed out that in her work "the symbol stamps the mind with an indelible impression and shows the poignance of meanings extracted from a depth of mind and consciousness that alone ensures a compelling form of truth."[9]

The full nature of the truth that can be revealed by symbol, by the subconscious, however, becomes more evident only as more is known about the subconscious, and Bogan's reviewers did not go into *what* her poetry says in any depth. They responded—those who did respond—also on a more or less subconscious level which they then tried to explain. The resultant obscurity found in the poems was attributed at times to concentration of style or to a private, too personal, content. Robert L. Wolf said of *Body of This Death:* "Where Miss Bogan is difficult—and she often is—it is because she has too much to say; it is because each word is pregnant with such extreme intensity that she has not woven language that will bear the burden."[10] Léonie Adams, in a later review (referring to Marianne Moore's review, "Compactness Compacted"), saw a different quality in the concentration of meaning: "It is not the concentration of density, dazzling or murky, to be found in some modern work, but of rapid elucidation, and its secret is again that of the poise of elements in the poem."[11]

The criticism sometimes voiced that Bogan should loosen her poetic structure, "deliver herself more luxuriously to her art," as Wolf put it, does not recognize that Bogan's poetry arose from the same psychological sources as the concentrated symbolism and imagery. It is the archetypal nature of the subconscious that gives art meaning to others than the creators, who may not understand all the implications themselves. It is relevant, I think, that reviewers of Bogan's poetry often modified a statement indicating that they did not understand what she was saying with a remark that the poetry did have important meaning, nevertheless. An illustration is a comment made by Mark Van Doren in a review of *Body of This Death:*

> Miss Bogan has spoken always with intensity and intelligent skill; she has not always spoken clearly. Now and then her poetry comes too immediately from a personal source to mean very much to others. Nevertheless, this first volume places her near the lead of those poets today—Ann Wickham, Charlotte Mew, Genevieve Taggard, and others—who are passionately exploring the endless, narrow paths of woman's (and man's) experience. It is absolutely individual, yet it reaches toward the race. It may be a classic.[12]

Bogan herself felt that "minor art needs to be hard, condensed and durable."[13] Morton Zabel thought so, too, and also felt that Bogan has achieved those qualities in her poetry:

> She has kept to the hardest line of integrity a poet can follow and has sacrificed the easier victories of many of her contemporaries. Her work, instinctive with self-criticism and emotional severity, speaks with one voice

only, her rewards and those of her readers have a common source in the discipline to which the clarity of her music and her unsophistic craftmanship
are a testimony. It should be a model for poets in any decade or of any
ambition. [14]

Such poetry is often difficult to understand. Zabel, himself, while
recognizing the search for psychological truth, did not seem to understand very much about the specific nature of the truth of the
poems. Roethke recognized that the poetry was not readily compre-
hensible simply because it meant so much. He said of the poems in
ending his Hopwood Lecture at the University of Michigan:

They are timeless, impersonal in a curious way and objective—not highly
idiosyncratic as so much of the best American work is. Her poems can be
read and reread: they keep yielding new meanings, as all good poetry
should. The ground beat of the great tradition can be heard, with the necessary subtle variations. Bogan is one of the true inheritors. Her poems create their own reality, and demand not just attention, but the emotional and
spiritual response of the whole man. Such a poet will never be popular, but
can and should be a true model for the young. And the best work will stay
in the language as long as the language survives. [15]

Whether the work stays in the language remains to be seen, but it
has survived a bypass in poetic style for the last forty or so years with
the consequent exclusion from many anthologies. There were always
those who valued Bogan's poetry, however. Auden, whose *The Crite-
rion Book of Modern American Verse* (1956) included two of her poems,
wrote her about her collection, *Poems and New Poems,* "Comparisons
are supposed to be odious, but I find the last half of your book a finer
body of work than any similar body of English lyrics of this century,
bar none."[16] Roethke was strongly influenced by Bogan. Sylvia Plath
in a letter to her mother (April 26, 1956) indicated her affinity for
Bogan when she mentioned that she was going to submit a book of
poems "to a board of judges (5), including the best poets and most
congenial to my style: Louise Bogan, Richard Wilbur, Rolfe Humphries, May Sarton, and one other."[17] Bogan's "Medusa," for instance, can be seen as an influence upon Plath.

May Sarton, too, valued her work. "Long before I ever saw her face
to face Louise Bogan, both as poet and critic, had been a key figure
for me. I bought *The Sleeping Fury* in 1937 when I was twenty-five
and my first book had just appeared. I can still remember the shock

and exhilaration it meant, how I pondered the poems—those strict spare lines, where emotion was so often disciplined by irony."[18] William Jay Smith writes, "It was the passionate intensity and control in her work that appealed to me." He bought *The Sleeping Fury* in 1938 and "read that book over and over night and day."[19]

Now interest is reviving in Bogan's poetry. The move to change the conditions that tend to exclude women from the arts has caused her work to be included in anthologies of women poets, for one thing. Florence Howe, in an introduction to *No More Masks!*, a 1973 anthology of poems by women, comments upon the difficulties experienced by women poets in previous years and their consequent hiding behind masculine or asexual masks:

> Yeats could write from his maleness when he chose, as could those allegedly "objective" artists, Eliot and Joyce. It is significant to note that women writers esteemed by men are not, on the whole, allowed similar privileges. Or, to put it another way, those women artists esteemed by men are not ones to declaim themselves women. Neither in puzzlement or pain (like [Amy] Lowell) nor in bitterness (like Louise Bogan).[20]

But now, she says, women poets "are bound together in ways Lowell, Bogan or Plath could not have imagined."[21] Because of this, and the interest aroused by the publication of Bogan's letters in 1973, young women—as well as other people of all ages and both sexes—are discovering and liking her poetry. Increasingly, her work is being studied and written about; and, as an indication of demand, *The Blue Estuaries* is again available in paperback.

I believe that as the cultural limitations that interfered with an understanding of Bogan's poetry increasingly diminish, she will come to be read and enjoyed by a wider audience than ever before. In 1968, in reviewing *The Blue Estuaries* for the *New York Times Book Review*, William Meredith began by saying, "There is no way to deal with Louise Bogan, one of the best women poets alive, without engaging the question of what it means to be a woman artist in a man's culture." Elaborating upon his statement, he said:

> It is this ambivalent prejudice that a woman artist must face—a culture that asks her, which are you, a poetess or a goddess, a little lady poet or a great-breasted, all-knowing mother? It is a question that makes "Have you stopped beating your wife?" seem quite guileless. Like the best artists of her sex, Miss Bogan has both disdained to answer it and given the right answer: I am an observant and feeling human being.

Of *The Blue Estuaries,* Meredith said: "Reading this book with delight, I was struck (as Roethke must have been in 1961) by how Louise Bogan's reputation has lagged behind a career of stubborn, individual excellence."[22]

That her reputation is reviving is evidenced again by Irving Howe in a 1978 review of *The Poetry Anthology: 1912–1977,* a collection of poems from *Poetry* magazine: "Edwin Arlington Robinson, Walter de la Mare, Louise Bogan and J. V. Cunningham, having kept their distance from the 'new poetry,' now seem brightly new."[23]

I believe that time will prove that the poetry of Louise Bogan has attained her goal of being "hard, condensed and durable."

Notes and References

Chapter One

    1. Collected in *A Poet's Alphabet: Reflections on the Literary Art and Vocation,* ed. Robert Phelps and Ruth Limmer (New York, 1970), p. 151. First given as a talk ("On the Pleasures of Formal Verse") at a poetry conference at Bard College in 1948. William Carlos Williams spoke in opposition.

    2. Ibid., p. 156.

    3. Ibid., p. 159. See Gilbert Murray, *The Classical Tradition in Poetry* (Cambridge, Mass.: Harvard University Press, 1927), p. 255.

    4. Examples: Bogan introduced a selection of her poems (on Tape LWO 2689, reel 2), reading at the Library of Congress, as the kind that would be attached to music, that have emotional impact. The manuscript of "Little Lobelia's Song" in the Bogan papers, Amherst College Library, has written at the top ". . . with supposed music." Sister Angela's (Veronica B. O'Reilly) "The Art of Louise Bogan" (University of San Diego, 1971), has a chapter on the musicality of Bogan's poetry, chapter 3, " 'Creative Architecture' Form and Structure," pp. 59–82.

    5. Susanne K. Langer, *Feeling and Form* (New York: Scribner's, 1953), p. 27.

    6. Letter of November 27, 1938, in *What the Woman Lived: Selected Letters of Louise Bogan 1920–1970,* ed. Ruth Limmer (New York: Harcourt Brace Jovanovich, 1973), p. 180; hereafter cited as *Letters*.

    7. September 19, 1966, *Letters,* p. 369.

    8. "The Situation in American Writing: Seven Questions (Part Two)," *Partisan Review* 6 (Fall 1939):105–8. The question in full is No. 1 on p. 103, and the reply in full is on p. 105. Excerpts are reprinted in *Journey Around My Room: The Autobiography of Louise Bogan,* A Mosaic by Ruth Limmer (New York, 1980), p. 217; hereafter cited as JAMR.

    9. Ibid., question No. 5 on p. 103, answered on pp. 106–7.

    10. Letter dated May 21, 1938, *Letters,* p. 170. The reference to the *Sacred Heart Messenger* is probably to the organ of the League of the Sacred Heart, a Roman Catholic group commonly known as the Apostleship of Prayer.

    11. Letter of March 4, 1941, *Letters,* p. 34n2.

    12. Letter of March 22, 1939, *Letters,* p. 185.

    13. Letter of August 6, 1924, *Letters,* p. 12.

    14. MS, fol. 5, New York Public Library, Berg Collection, Letters to May Sarton.

15. "The Heart and the Lyre," *A Poet's Alphabet*, p. 428. An interesting discussion of Bogan's views of women is given by Gloria Bowles in "Louise Bogan: To Be (or Not to Be?) Woman Poet," *Women's Studies* 5, no. 2 (1977):131–35.

16. *A Poet's Alphabet*, p. 432. The title refers to a work by the nineteenth-century French poet Paul Verlaine, "Les Poètes Maudits" ("The Damned Poets") in which he discusses six poets—including himself—who pursued their art at odds with society.

17. Elder Olson, "Louise Bogan and Léonie Adams," *Chicago Review* 8 (Fall 1954):70–87, also comments upon the nature of love for the persona in Bogan's poems.

18. In a letter to Theodore Roethke, October 1935, she writes, "I hate authority" (*Letters*, p. 113).

19. In a letter to Sister Angela, July 5, 1969, Bogan says, "You will remember, I'm sure, in dealing with my work, that you are dealing with emotion under high pressure—so that *symbols* are its only release" (*Letters*, p. 92n3).

20. In an explanatory leaflet to "July Dawn" (San Francisco: Poems in Folio, 1957), she discussed the lyric gift and the creative process.

21. MS, Amherst College Library, Bogan Papers.

22. *The Blue Estuaries: Poems 1923–1968* (New York, 1968), p. 3; hereafter page references cited in the text. This is Louise Bogan's last and approved collection.

23. *Body of This Death* (New York, 1923), p. 25.

24. Letter to John Hall Wheelock, July 28, 1941, *Letters*, p. 222. However, the poem was published again later in *Voices*, no. 146 (September-December 1951):9.

25. Bogan mentioned Fletcher's poem as the source of the title on Library of Congress Tape LWO 5504, reel 1. Ms. Limmer wrote me on July 20, 1975: "I own her [Bogan's] copy of *The English Galaxy of Shorter Poems* in the Everyman edition, and she fox-eared the page on which appears Fletcher's 'Come, Sleep, and with thy sweet deceiving. . . .' So I have always assumed that this Fletcher poem is the source of her title. The *English Galaxy* was an anthology of which she was very, very fond."

26. On Tape LWO 5504, reel 2, in the Library of Congress Recorded Sound Division.

Chapter Two

1. "The Situation in American Writing: Seven Questions (Part Two)," *Partisan Review* 6:105.

2. F. 2, New York City Public Library, Berg Collection, May Sarton Letters.

3. Letter to May Sarton, May 23, 1954, *Letters*, p. 288.

4. April 15, 1936, *Letters*, pp. 129–30.

5. "American Literature," in *A Poet's Alphabet*, p. 14.

6. Letter of August 23, 1935, *Letters*, pp. 96–97.

7. Letter of July 2, 1935, *Letters*, p. 91.

8. Letter of July 28, 1941, *Letters*, p. 222. Elizabeth P. Perlmutter comments upon Bogan's rejection in her mature poetry of what Perlmutter calls "the Girl" in "A Doll's Heart: The Girl in the Poetry of Edna St. Vincent Millay and Louise Bogan," *Twentieth Century Literature* 23 (1977):157–79.

9. Note by Ruth Limmer in *Letters*, p. 8.

10. Letter October 16, 1934, and n1 by Ruth Limmer (*Letters*, p. 82).

11. The relationship of this poem to Yeats's "The Wild Swans at Coole" is discussed in chapter 5.

12. Genevieve Taggard lists "The Alchemist," "Chanson Un Peu Naive," and "Women" by Louise Bogan in her book *Circumference: Varieties of Metaphysical Verse 1456–1928* (New York: Covici Friede Publishers, 1929).

13. "Poetry," in *America Now*, ed. Harold E. Stearns (New York: C. Scribner's Sons, 1938), p. 55.

14. *A Poet's Alphabet*, p. 130.

15. *Poet's Choice*, ed. Paul Engle and Joseph Langland (New York: Dial Press, 1962), p. 32; JAMR, p. 118.

16. Joseph E. Duncan, *The Revival of Metaphysical Poetry: The History of a Style, 1800 to the Present* (Minneapolis: University of Minnesota Press, 1959), p. 205.

Chapter Three

1. "A Carol," Boston University *Beacon*, Christmas 1915, p. 210, "The Betrothal of King Cophetua," April 1916, p. 298. The second poem was reprinted in *Anthology of Boston University Poetry* (New York: Colony Press, 1931), p. 36.

2. Bogan mentioned in a letter to Allen Tate of February 19, 1927 (*Letters*, pp. 33–34), that she had come across the name "Bowghan" in one of the ballads of Percy's *Reliques;* and William Jay Smith speaks of her early acquaintance with Tennyson in *Louise Bogan: A Woman's Words* (Washington, D.C.: Library of Congress, 1971), p. 11.

3. Letter of February 16, 1954, *Letters*, p. 285.

4. *Others* 4 (December 1917). "Betrothed" is on p. 10 and "The Young Wife" on pp. 11–13.

5. *Poetry: A Magazine of Verse* 20 (August 1922):248–51.

6. *Liberator* 6, no. 5 (May 1923):14. Reprinted in *May Days, An Anthology of Verse from Masses—Liberator,* ed. Genevieve Taggard (New York: Boni and Liveright, 1925), p. 202.

Chapter Four

1. *Body of This Death* (New York, 1923). Page numbers in the text refer to *The Blue Estuaries*.

2. Arthur Symons, *The Symbolist Movement in Literature,* 3d rev. ed. (1899; rpt. New York: Dutton, 1958), p. 70.

3. In a letter to Sister Angela of August 20, 1966, Bogan remarked of a poem of this period ("Juan's Song"), "I think one can detect the bitterness which comes with a breakdown of early idealism." The letter is reproduced in Sister Angela's thesis and in *Letters,* p. 368.

4. *Body of This Death,* p. 18.

5. Sister Angela, "The Art of Louise Bogan," p. 11.

6. Ibid., p. 57.

7. "Journey Around My Room," *New Yorker,* January 14, 1933, pp. 17–18. Bogan took her title from *Voyage Autour de ma Chambre* by Xavier de Maistre, the eighteenth-century French writer. Bogan's piece is used by Ruth Limmer as the frame for JAMR.

8. "Dove and Serpent," *New Yorker,* November 18, 1933, pp. 24–26. Reprinted in JAMR, pp. 3–8.

9. Letter March 23, 1934, *Letters,* pp. 77–79. There is a footnote to the letter by Ruth Limmer that says: "LB worked at this prose piece occasionally all through her life. The only surviving fragment—handwritten on yellow foolscap sheets—was dated June 1959."

10. "Dove and Serpent," pp. 24–25; hereafter cited in the text as *DS*.

11. Old Leonard was probably referring to Matthew 10:16: "Behold, I send you forth as sheep in the midst of wolves: be ye therefore wise as serpents and harmless as doves."

12. Letter of July 5, 1969. In Sister Angela's thesis, p. 123.

13. R. L. Wolf, "Impassioned Austerity," *Poetry: A Magazine of Verse,* no. 23 (March 1924):335.

14. Bogan referred to "Juan's Song" as an early poem in the letter to Sister Angela of August 20, 1966.

15. See note 3 above. "Juan's Song" was first published in the *New Yorker,* May 24, 1930, p. 28.

16. *Measure,* no. 39 (May 1924):10. The title was changed to "Girl's Song" when the poem was collected in *Dark Summer* and is on p. 35 of *The Blue Estuaries*.

17. *Body of This Death,* pp. 5–7.

18. Letter of July 28, 1941, *Letters,* p. 222. "A Letter" is reprinted in JAMR, pp. 70–72.

19. *Body of This Death,* pp. 10–11.

20. "Reading Contemporary Poetry," *English Journal,* February 1953, p. 59.

21. See "From the Journals of a Poet," ed. Ruth Limmer, *New Yorker,* January 30, 1978, pp. 39–42, and *Journey Around My Room.*
22. Letter of June 11, 1937, *Letters,* p. 6n2.
23. "The Springs of Poetry," *New Republic,* December 5, 1923, pt. 2, p. 9. See JAMR, p. 70.

Chapter Five

1. July 24, 1924, *Letters,* p. 9.
2. August 24, 1924, *Letters,* p. 13.
3. August 25, 1925, *Letters,* pp. 22–23.
4. April 9, 1926, *Letters,* p. 27. As Ruth Limmer explains in notes on p. 5 (no. 2) and p. 18 (no. 2), Margaret Mead hired poets to help catalog when she was an assistant to a professor of sociology at Columbia University. Mead tried her hand at poetry, too, and wrote a poem about Bogan entitled "To a Proud Lady" (published in *Measure,* June 1925, p. 16). Ruth Benedict also wrote poetry.
5. *Dark Summer* (New York, 1929). Page numbers in the text refer to *The Blue Estuaries.*
6. July 24, 1924, *Letters,* p. 9.
7. TS, Box XIII, F. 3, Bogan Papers.
8. See the letter from Bogan to Wheelock of December 7, 1928, *Letters,* p. 40.
9. In a review of Howard Nemerov's *New and Selected Poems* (1961); *A Poet's Alphabet,* p. 227.
10. Yvor Winters, "The Poetry of Louise Bogan," *New Republic* 60 (October 16, 1929):247.
11. Theodore Roethke, "The Poetry of Louise Bogan," *Michigan Quarterly Review* 6 (Autumn 1967):246; hereafter cited as *MQR* in text.
12. Ford Madox Ford, "The Flame in Stone," *Poetry* 50 (June 1937):161.
13. The swan is also a symbol used by Baudelaire and Mallarmé, as both Yeats and Bogan were undoubtedly aware.
14. *The Collected Poems of W. B. Yeats* (New York: Macmillan Co., 1956), pp. 129–30.
15. In a letter to Sister Angela of August 20, 1966, she said, " 'The Mark' . . . is much more contemplative" (*Letters,* p. 368).
16. *Letters,* p. 24.
17. Box 30, F. 8. University of Chicago, *Poetry* Magazine Papers (1912–36).
18. *New Yorker,* May 22, 1926, p. 56.
19. *New Yorker,* December 14, 1929, p. 35.

20. In a review of *American Poetry,* ed. G. W. Allen, W. B. Rideout, and J. K. Robinson (1966); *A Poet's Alphabet,* p. 29.

21. Library of Congress Tape LWO 2689, reel 2.

22. *Dark Summer,* pp. 19–29.

23. *Letters,* p. 8.

24. July 24, 1924, *Letters,* p. 9. Bogan apparently was also responding to another fear. She later wrote in her journal, "My mother was afraid of the flume. It had voices for her: it called her and beckoned her. So I, too, began to fear it" ("From the Journals of a Poet," p. 47); JAMR, p. 60. "The Flume" is reprinted in JAMR, pp. 60–67.

25. August 28, 1924, *Letters,* p. 14.

26. To Rolfe Humphries, *Letters,* p. 15.

27. On Library of Congress Tape LWO 2869, reel 2, Bogan calls the poem "a short poem which is a memory of childhood."

28. "Louise Bogan Reads Her Works," Yale Series of Recorded Poets, Carillon Records YP 308 (1961). Critical notes by Harold Bloom on the slipcase. Further comments on "Summer Wish" by Bloom are from this same source.

29. May Sarton, "Louise Bogan," in *A World of Light: Portraits and Celebrations* (New York, 1976), p. 233.

30. In a letter to May Sarton of October 15, 1954, *Letters,* p. 291.

31. Louis Untermeyer comments that in *Dark Summer,* Bogan "pierces reality to the secret behind appearance" (*Saturday Review of Literature,* February 1, 1930, p. 692).

32. Sister Angela, "The Art of Louise Bogan," p. 29.

Chapter Six

1. January 6, 1930, *Letters,* p. 55.

2. MS, Box XX, F. 2, Bogan Papers.

3. Letter to Harriet Monroe, October 24, 1930, and note by Ruth Limmer, *Letters,* pp. 56–57.

4. Box XIII, Bogan Papers.

5. "Keramik," in *The American Caravan: A Yearbook of American Literature* (New York: Macaulay, 1927), pp. 673–78.

6. "Art Embroidery," *New Republic,* March 21, 1928, p. 156.

7. "The Last Tear," *New Yorker,* July 22, 1933, p. 22.

8. "Sabbatical Summer," *New Yorker,* July 11, 1931, pp. 18–21.

9. "A Speakeasy Life," *New Yorker,* August 29, 1931, pp. 14–16.

10. Box XIII, F. 8, Bogan Papers.

11. TS, Box XIII, F. 7, Bogan Papers.

12. TS, Box XIII, F. 10, Bogan Papers.

13. "Sunday at Five," *New Yorker,* December 12, 1931, p. 19.

14. "Conversation Piece," *New Yorker*, August 12, 1933, pp. 13–14. Reprinted in *Short Stories from the New Yorker* (New York: Simon & Schuster, 1945), pp. 141–44.

15. "Letdown," *New Yorker*, October 20, 1934, pp. 18–20. See JAMR, pp. 38–43.

16. "To Take Leave," *New Yorker*, January 26, 1935, pp. 26–27. See JAMR, pp. 127–29.

17. TS, Box XIII, F. 11.

18. *Letters*, p. 71.

19. TS, Box XIII, F. 5.

20. "Hydrotherapy," *New Yorker*, June 27, 1931, p. 18.

21. "The Short Life of Emily," *New Yorker*, May 6, 1933, pp. 17–18.

22. "Zest," *New Yorker*, October 24, 1931, pp. 16–19.

23. *The Sleeping Fury* (New York, 1937), p. 12; *The Blue Estuaries*, p. 70.

24. "Coming Out," *New Yorker*, October 14, 1933, p. 22. See also JAMR, pp. 79–82.

25. TS, Box XIII, F. 6, Bogan Papers. "The Long Walk" is in JAMR, pp. 85–90.

26. Bogan once wrote: "The poet represses the outright narrative of his life. He absorbs it, along with life itself. The repressed becomes the poem. Actually, I have written down my experience in the closest detail. But the rough and vulgar facts are not there" ("From the Journals of a Poet," p. 62).

Chapter Seven

1. August 25, 1925, *Letters*, p. 22.

2. Letter to Harriet Monroe of October 14, 1932, University of Chicago Library, Box 30, F. 8, *Poetry* Magazine Papers.

3. Letter of March 15, 1933: "I plan to sail early in April for Genoa, and go down to Sicily before I visit Florence, the hill towns and Venice" (*Letters*, p. 73).

4. June 12, 1933, *Letters*, p. 75.

5. Letter to Katharine S. White, January 1934, *Letters*, pp. 76–77.

6. August 22, 1934, *Letters*, p. 81.

7. Letter to Morton Zabel, February 5, 1935, *Letters*, p. 83.

8. Letter of March 16, 1954, May Sarton Papers, F. 4.

9. J. B. Leishman, trans., *Rainer Maria Rilke: Poems* (London: Hogarth Press, 1934), p. 20. I have not used the identical wording of Leishman's translation.

10. *Letters*, pp. 86–87.

11. Ruth Limmer told me in a letter of July 20, 1975, that Bogan was *always* translating Rilke.

12. July 27, 1934, *Letters,* p. 78.

13. Letter to Morton Zabel, August 27, 1933, *Letters,* p. 76.

14. Letter to Zabel, December 8, 1936, *Letters,* p. 145.

15. MS, Box XI, F. 62, Bogan Papers. Letter to John Hall Wheelock, June 1936, *Letters,* p. 132.

16. "The Springs of Poetry," p. 9.

17. *The Sleeping Fury.* Page numbers in the text refer to *The Blue Estuaries,* where this appears on p. 65.

18. TS, Box XI, F. 61, Bogan Papers.

19. Letter to Zabel, November 29, 1932, *Letters,* p. 69.

20. Letter to John Wheelock, October 31, 1932, as Ruth Limmer explains in note 3, *Letters,* p. 71.

21. Letter to Rolfe Humphries, February 1936, *Letters,* p. 127.

22. TS with penciled comments by Edmund Wilson, no date, Box XI, F. 19, Bogan Papers.

23. In the letter to Zabel, ". . . called 'Exhortation' or perhaps, 'All Souls' Eve' " (*Letters,* p. 69).

24. TS, Box 30, F. 8, *Poetry* Magazine Papers.

25. May 2, 1931, *Letters,* p. 58.

26. June 23, 1931 (*Letters,* p. 59), and letter to Allen Tate, October 8, 1931, p. 60.

27. June 23, 1931, *Letters,* p. 59.

28. *New Yorker,* February 1, 1930, p. 17.

29. *New Yorker,* January 3, 1931, p. 21; JAMR, p. 69.

30. *New Yorker,* May 28, 1932, p. 20.

31. "Italian Morning," though first published in 1935 in *Scribner's* magazine, was likely written earlier (see *Letters,* p. 86).

32. Letter to John Wheelock, July 1935, *Letters,* p. 86.

33. October 28, 1936, *Letters,* p. 138.

34. July 2, 1935, *Letters,* pp. 88–92.

35. *Letters,* p. 89.

36. MS, Box XI, F. 2, Bogan Papers.

37. "Hidden," *New Yorker,* February 15, 1936, p. 20; and "To My Brother," *New Yorker,* October 26, 1935, p. 31.

38. Letter to Roethke, October 3, 1935, *Letters,* p. 108. The MSS of "Hidden" and "To My Brother" are among the Bogan Papers.

39. TS of "We Might Have Striven Years" is dated 1935, Box XI, F. 75; TS of "When at Last" is in F. 76.

40. Library of Congress Tape LWO 2869, reel 2. The museum was identified as the Museo delle Terme in Rome when "The Sleeping Fury" was published in *Poetry* (see note 42 below).

41. MS, Box XI, F. 62, Bogan Papers. There are several versions but they are unnumbered.

42. *Poetry* magazine, December 1936, pp. 119–23.

43. Letter of November 6, 1935, *Letters,* p. 116.
44. Letter to John Wheelock, July 29, 1936, *Letters,* p. 133n2.
45. Letter to J. Wheelock, June 1936, *Letters,* p. 132.
46. TS, MS, Box XI, F. 57, Bogan Papers.
47. Letter of December 1935, *Letters,* p. 122.
48. Yeats, *Collected Poems,* p. 452.
49. "The Cutting of an Agate," *Nation* 148 (February 25, 1939):234. In *A Poet's Alphabet,* p. 463.
50. A journal entry of January 12, 1954, refers to "the packet of letters" as Raymond's letters and cables to her and her letters to him—both the love letters of 1933 and the ones written after the separation. She describes her sense of being trapped, used, and made an object. "From the Journals of a Poet," p. 41. See JAMR, pp. 125–27.
51. November 14, 1936, *Letters,* p. 142.
52. November 1936, as R. Limmer explains, *Letters,* p. 143n1.
53. Letter to J. Wheelock, October 28, 1936, *Letters,* p. 138.

Chapter Eight

1. Letters to Zabel, December 27, 1936, and to R. Humphries, January 18, 1937, *Letters,* pp. 147, 150.
2. September 1937, *Letters,* p. 163.
3. Letter to Zabel, August 22, 1940, *Letters,* p. 209.
4. Letter of July 12, 1937, *Letters,* p. 157.
5. *Letters,* p. 207.
6. Letter of February 24, 1941, *Letters,* p. 215.
7. TS, Box XI, F. 54, Bogan Papers.
8. *Nation,* August 7, 1937, p. 153. Reprinted in *Journey Around My Room,* p. 106.
9. *Poetry,* October 1937, p. 3.
10. *Poems and New Poems* (New York, 1941), p. 95; *The Blue Estuaries,* p. 93. Page numbers in the text hereafter refer to *The Blue Estuaries.*
11. Earl Daniels, "Explication: 'Solitary Observations,' " in *The Art of Reading Poetry* (New York: Farrar & Rinehart, 1941), pp. 199–200.
12. *New Republic* 103 (December 9, 1940):803–4.
13. Library of Congress Tape LWO 5504, reel 2.
14. August 20, 1966, *Letters,* p. 368.
15. August 14, 1954, *Letters,* p. 369n2.
16. Stanley Kunitz, "Pentagons and Pomegranates," *Poetry* 60 (April 1942):42–43.
17. November 13, 1929, *Letters,* p. 50.
18. According to Bogan on Library of Congress Tape LWO 5504, reel 1. Bogan's poem has been set to music by Samuel Barber, Op. 42, no. 2 (New York: G. Schirmer, 1969), octavo no. 111644.

19. *Nation* 147 (December 10, 1938):624–25. The other parodies were "Imitation of a Novel (or a Prose Poem) by Kay Boyle," "Imitation of a Poem by Frederick Prokosch," and "Empty Lyrics: Plain, Fancy."

20. John Malcolm Brinnin and Bill Read, eds., *The Modern Poets* (New York: McGraw Hill, 1963), p. 44.

21. In a letter to R. Humphries, November 27, 1938: "We are all self-lovers to an almost complete degree" (*Letters,* p. 180).

22. November 13, 1959, *Letters,* p. 317.

23. T. S. Eliot, "Three Voices of Poetry," in *On Poetry and Poets* (New York: Noonday Press, 1961), p. 107.

Chapter Nine

1. October 14, 1948, *Letters,* p. 262.

2. *Voices: A Quarterly of Poetry,* September-December 1951, p. 8.

3. Letter of January 19, 1952, *Letters,* p. 277.

4. James Elroy Flecker's *The Golden Journey to Samarkand* (London: Max Goschen, 1913) could well have influenced the imagery of both poems. Bogan liked the poem when very young and included the "Prologue" in the anthology of poems for young people that she edited with William Jay Smith. They named the anthology *The Golden Journey* after Flecker's poem.

5. Letter of February 4, 1954, *Letters,* p. 283.

6. *Collected Poems 1923–1953* (New York, 1954, pp. 122–24. *The Blue Estuaries,* pp. 115–17. Page numbers in the text refer to *The Blue Estuaries.*

7. The text of the poem in *Collected Poems* has the word *voice* rather than *face* in the line between the first and second stanzas. Although the error was noted in an erratum, it was carried over without correction into the 1968 edition of *The Blue Estuaries.* It is corrected in the Ecco Press edition.

8. MS, Box XI, F. 64, Bogan Papers.

9. Rolfe Humphries changed the poem from four stanzas to three stanzas, according to Ruth Limmer (*Letters,* p. 267n1). William Jay Smith discusses the process of writing "Song for the Last Act" in "The Making of Poems," in *The Streaks of the Tulip* (New York: Delacorte Press, 1972), pp. 397–99. He says that Bogan told him that the poem lay in a folder for years before she put it in its final shape.

Chapter Ten

1. *Poetry,* October-November 1962, pp. 12–13.

2. June 12, 1963, *Letters,* pp. 362–63. See JAMR, pp. 45–48.

3. Bogan also, with May Sarton, translated some poems by Valéry, published in *The Hudson Review* and *Poetry* in 1959. See *Letters,* pp. 303 and 304n1.

4. The MS is dated September 20, 1961; Box XI, F. 11, Bogan Papers.
5. *Poetry in Crystal,* Steuben Glass (New York: Spiral Press, 1963), p. 18. Listed in Couchman bibliography.
6. October 22, 1961, *Letters,* p. 332.
7. MS is dated "crica 1940, re-written 1956 (Nov.)." Box XI, F. 58, Bogan Papers. In "Poets on Painting," *Art News,* September 1958, p. 24.
8. In *The Writer and His Craft,* Hopwood Lectures, 1932–52, ed. Robert Morss Lovett (Ann Arbor: University of Michigan Press, 1954), pp. 173–90.
9. In a letter to Zabel of April 1, 1940, "I . . . have written another called 'The Sorcerer's Daughter.' " *Letters,* p. 206. MS, "The Young Mage," dated October 9, 1957, Box XI, F. 79, Bogan Papers. "The American Imagination," *Times Literary Supplement,* November 6, 1959, p. xxiv.
10. MS, Box XI, F. 37, Bogan Papers.
11. Letter of February 16, 1957, *Letters,* p. 308.
12. Dated MS, Box XI, F. 30, Bogan Papers.
13. MS, Box XI, F. 40, Bogan Papers.
14. *Letters,* p. 308.
15. *Letters,* p. 309n1.
16. *New Yorker,* April 1, 1961, p. 45.
17. Letter of January 25, 1967, *Letters,* p. 371.
18. Letter of July 25, 1966, *Letters,* p. 368.
19. MS, Box XI, F. 56, Bogan Papers.
20. MS, Box XI, F. 38, Bogan Papers. See *Letters,* p. 372n2.
21. Gregory Bateson, *Mind and Nature: A Necessary Unity* (New York: E. P. Dutton, 1979), p. 88.

Chapter Eleven

1. Roethke, "The Poetry of Louise Bogan," p. 246.
2. Olson, "Louise Bogan and Léonie Adams," pp. 73–74.
3. Ford, "The Flame in Stone," p. 159.
4. Eda Lou Walton, "Henceforth from the Mind," *Nation* 144 (April 24, 1937):488.
5. John Ciardi, "Two Nuns and a Strolling Player," *Nation* 178 (May 22, 1954):445–46.
6. Richard Eberhart, "Common Charms from Deep Sources," *New York Times Book Review,* May 30, 1954, p. 6.
7. Hayden Carruth, "A Balance Exactly Struck," *Poetry,* August 1969, pp. 330–31.
8. "The Poetry of Louise Bogan," Roethke, pp. 248–51.
9. Morton Zabel, "Lyric Authority," *New Republic* 90 (May 5, 1937):391.

10. Wolf, "Impassioned Austerity," p. 337.

11. Leonie Adams, "All Has Been Translated into Treasure," *Poetry* 85 (December 1954):168.

12. Mark Van Doren, "Louise Bogan," *Nation* 117 (October 31, 1923):494.

13. Letter to Rolfe Humphries, January 24, 1936, *Letters,* p. 125.

14. Zabel, "Lyric Authority," pp. 391–92.

15. Roethke, "The Poetry of Louise Bogan," p. 251.

16. *Letters,* p. 226.

17. Sylvia Plath, *Letters Home* (New York: Harper & Row, 1975), p. 242.

18. Sarton, *A World of Light,* p. 215.

19. William Jay Smith, *Louise Bogan: A Woman's Words* (Washington, D.C.: Library of Congress, 1971), p. 5.

20. Florence Howe and Ellen Bass, eds., *No More Masks!* (Garden City, N.Y.: Anchor Press, 1973), p. 7.

21. Ibid., p. 33.

22. William Meredith, "Poems of a Human Being," *New York Times Book Review,* October 13, 1968, p. 4.

23. Irving Howe, "A Radical Turning," *New York Times Book Review,* November 19, 1978, p. 55.

Selected Bibliography

PRIMARY SOURCES

1. Poetry
The Blue Estuaries: Poems 1923–1968. New York: Farrar, Straus and Giroux, 1968. Reprint. New York: Ecco Press, 1977.
Body of This Death. New York: McBride, 1923.
Collected Poems 1923–1953. New York: Noonday, 1954.
Dark Summer. New York: Scribner's, 1929.
Poems and New Poems. New York: Scribner's, 1941.
The Sleeping Fury. New York: Scribner's, 1937.

2. Criticism
Achievement in American Poetry 1900–1950. Twentieth-Century Literature in America Series. Chicago: Henry Regnery, 1951.
A Poet's Alphabet: Reflections on the Literary Art and Vocation. Edited by Robert Phelps and Ruth Limmer. New York: McGraw-Hill, 1970.
Selected Criticism: Poetry and Prose. New York: Noonday, 1955.

3. Letters and Journals
Journey Around My Room: The Autobiography of Louise Bogan. A Mosaic by Ruth Limmer. New York: Viking Press, 1980.

4. Translations
With Elizabeth Mayer
Elective Affinities by Goethe. Chicago: Henry Regnery Co., 1963.
The Glass Bees by Ernst Juenger. New York: Noonday, 1960.
The Sorrows of Young Werther and *Novella* by Goethe. New York: Random House, 1971.
With Elizabeth Roget
The Journal of Jules Renard. New York: George Braziller, 1964.

5. Anthology
With William Jay Smith
The Golden Journey: Poems for Young People. Chicago: Reilly and Lee, 1965.

6. Documents in Collections
Amherst College Library, Louise Bogan Papers

New York Public Library, Berg Collection, Letters to May Sarton
University of Chicago, *Poetry* Magazine Papers (1912–36)

7. Recordings
"Louise Bogan Reads Her Works." Yale Series of Recorded Poets. Carillon
    Records YP 308 (1961). Critical notes by Harold Bloom on the
    slipcase.
Library of Congress Tape LWO 2689, reel 2.
Library of Congress Tape LWO 5504, reels 1 and 2.
Library of Congress Tape LWO 2869, reel 2.

SECONDARY SOURCES

1. Bibliography
Couchman, Jane. "Louise Bogan: A Bibliography of Primary and Second-
    ary Materials, 1915–1975." *Bulletin of Bibliography* 33, no. 2 (Febru-
    ary-March 1976):73–77, 104; 33, no. 3 (April-June 1976):111–26,
    147; and 32, no. 3 (July-September 1976):178–81.

2. Books
Frank, Elizabeth P. [Perlmutter]. *Louise Bogan: A Portrait.* New York:
    Knopf, 1985.

3. Articles and Parts of Books
Bowles, Gloria. "Louise Bogan: To Be (or Not to Be?) Woman Poet."
    Women's Studies 5, no. 2 (1977):131–35. A discussion of the role that
    repressive societal attitudes toward women poets played in Bogan's de-
    velopment as a poet. Bowles argues that Bogan's moving away from the
    subjective to the objective in her poetry was a result of her not consid-
    ering her experience as a woman to be worthy poetic matter.
Perlmutter, Elizabeth P. "A Doll's Heart: The Girl in the Poetry of Edna
    St. Vincent Millay and Louise Bogan." *Twentieth Century Literature* 23
    (May 1977):157–79. A comparison of the early work of Millay and Bo-
    gan in which the persona of the Girl is discussed as it operates in the
    poems of both writers. Perlmutter sees Bogan as deriving subject mat-
    ter and inspiration from Millay but going beyond her in developing a
    persona of maturity and complexity.
Roethke, Theodore. "The Poetry of Louise Bogan." *Michigan Quarterly Re-
    view* 6 (Autumn 1967):246–51. Roethke's 1960 Hopwood Lecture at
    the University of Michigan. He evaluates Bogan's poetry in terms of
    range of subject, imagery, language, and rhythm and finds her a strong
    poet.

Sarton, May. "Louise Bogan." In *A World of Light: Portraits and Celebrations*. New York: Norton, 1976. In this collection of essays about friends who have influenced her, fellow poet May Sarton describes Louise Bogan as poet and friend during the many years that she knew her. It is a personal view that offers some insight into the psychic demons that plagued Bogan.

Swafford, Russell Anne, and Paul Ramsey. "The Influence of Sara Teasdale on Louise Bogan." *CEA Critic* 41, no. 4 (1979):7–12. A comparison of the poetry of Sara Teasdale and Louise Bogan in which the authors see the poets as being in the lyric tradition and as being both alike and different. They believe Bogan to have been influenced by the older poet and discuss specific poems as examples.

Index